IN SEASON

In Season

Homilies through the Liturgical Year

LUKE TIMOTHY JOHNSON

CASCADE Books · Eugene, Oregon

IN SEASON
Homilies through the Liturgical Year

Copyright © 2021 Luke Timothy Johnson. All rights reserved. Except for brief quotations in critical publications or reviews, no part of this book may be reproduced in any manner without prior written permission from the publisher. Write: Permissions, Wipf and Stock Publishers, 199 W. 8th Ave., Suite 3, Eugene, OR 97401.

Cascade Books
An Imprint of Wipf and Stock Publishers
199 W. 8th Ave., Suite 3
Eugene, OR 97401

www.wipfandstock.com

PAPERBACK ISBN: 978-1-7252-9532-2
HARDCOVER ISBN: 978-1-7252-9531-5
EBOOK ISBN: 978-1-7252-9533-9

Cataloguing-in-Publication data:

Names: Johnson, Luke Timothy, author.
Title: In season : homilies for the liturgical year / by Luke Timoty Johnson.
Description: Eugene, OR: Cascade Books, 2021 | Includes bibliographical references.
Identifiers: ISBN 978-1-7252-9532-2 (paperback) | ISBN 978-1-7252-9531-5 (hardcover) | ISBN 978-1-7252-9533-9 (ebook)
Subjects: LCSH: Church year sermons. | Sermons, American—20th century. | Sermons, American—21st century.
Classification: BX1756 J64 2021 (paperback) | BX1756 (ebook)

09/24/21

CONTENTS

Introduction | vii

ADVENT TO CHRISTMAS
The Season of Crisis | 3
The Coming of the Lord | 8
Hope and Commitment | 11
Christmas Present | 14
The Mystery That Is Christmas | 17
Shaped by the Word | 20

LENT
Fasting and Dieting | 25
The Old and New Adam | 28
Light and Life | 32
Avarice the Deadly Sin | 36
Repentance | 40

HOLY WEEK
The Cross and Christian Existence | 47
The Power of the Cross | 52
Jesus's Faith and Ours | 57
The Table of the Lord | 61
Putting the Body Where the Mouth Is | 65
Speaking Truth in Face of Deceit | 71

GOOD FRIDAY
Prayer and Suffering | 79
Simple Not Easy | 82
Revelatory Death | 89
The Suffering Servant | 93
The Body Language of Love | 98

EASTER TO CHRIST THE KING
The Day of Resurrection | 105
Paradoxical Life | 109
Dying We Live | 114
The Easter Presence of Jesus | 118
The Childless Kingdom | 122
The Eucharist and the Identity of Jesus | 127
Transfigurations | 136
Clothed with Christ | 141
God the Comic | 144

SAINTS AND ANGELS
Foundation of Faith | 149
The Cost of Witnessing | 152
The Angelic Host | 155
We Live by Faith | 159
The Blessed and the Blasé | 164

INTRODUCTION

Preaching sermons was not something I did by choice but by necessity. When I became a Benedictine monk in 1963, I wanted only to live my life according to the *Rule of Benedict* and praise God through the chanting of the psalms. But I also wanted to be a scholar. And at that time, being a full choir monk, and having scholarship as one's main work rather than milking cows, meant becoming an ordained priest. With the priesthood came the obligation to preach—to my community and to the congregations that would attend the monastic Eucharist. Thus, although I never then or since thought of myself as a preacher, I guess I became one of sorts.

The monastic life is one defined by the ancient liturgical life of the church. The seasons of the year from Advent to Advent indelibly shape the consciousness of monks. Preaching in the monastic context, then, naturally meant reading and interpreting Scripture within the context of the liturgical season. The main liturgical cycle is "seasonal." Each year, the church follows and celebrates the path of salvation revealed in Scripture from the expectation of the Messiah in Advent to the time of the church in the Sundays following Pentecost. A secondary cycle is called "sanctoral." Virtually every day of the year remembers a martyr, confessor, virgin, or teacher through whom God's spirit of transformation was manifested.

All the sermons in this slender book are closer to homilies than to formal sermons. The Greek word from which "homily" derives suggests a conversation. This casual, relaxed, and everyday sort of rhetoric perfectly fits the setting of a community worshiping together and hearing one of its members reflect on the day and its readings.

I carried much of that style with me when I left the monastery and the priesthood in 1972. But why and how did I end up still preaching? As a professor of New Testament at Yale Divinity School from 1976–1982 and at the Candler School of Theology from 1992–2016, I was expected to take my turn as a preacher at student worship. I also preached by invitation at local

INTRODUCTION

congregations around the country. During the 20 years when I was *persona non grata* within Catholicism, these sermons were given almost entirely to Protestant congregations.

I always found the task of preaching to be at once terrifying and exhilarating. Terrifying, because in sharp contrast to teaching, which enables one to stand apart from the text or subject and talk about it, preaching demands that the preacher stand under the judgment of the word together with those to whom he speaks, and work through the text and the moment. When this shift is made, one is aware that one is answerable to the Living God, and not simply the approval of the congregation. But also, exhilarating, because, unlike most teaching of Scripture, preaching demanded and invited a direct and edifying appropriation of the text in relation to life. No footnotes, no learned asides, nothing but the text, the moment, and (one always hopes) the Spirit of the Living God enlivening one's mind to explore and discover dimensions of the text and the moment that scholarship could never reach.

Unlike the ease I always felt when teaching, therefore, I found preaching to be spiritually and emotionally difficult, primarily because, for the most part, it was "celebrity preaching." I was often not speaking to my own community but to strangers who shared nothing with me except our faith and the liturgical action. They often had high expectations of a preacher/teacher whom they had invited to teach and preach. Thus, despite my deepest longing to be simple and transparent to the text, I found that my shyness required me to write out my sermons, and once I started writing, the desire to write prettily came into conflict with the longing for simplicity. I consequently did not ever really enjoy the act of preaching in the way I did teaching.

As it turned out, though, I ended up delivering quite a few sermons. Not all of them are worth making available to a wider audience. You may think that some of these should not have made the cut. My selection of these homilies was based on their liturgical connection. Each of them in some way fits within the church's seasonal and sanctoral cycle. As in all my preaching, I followed the church's lectionary.

You will see that they vary a great deal in length. But although they were given over a period of some fifty years, you will also see, I think, that the voice stays fairly constant. Two oddities that should be flagged. First, in some of my sermons, I could only break through my psychological resistance to preaching by using the form of verse, or something that looks like

INTRODUCTION

verse. I have kept that format here. Indeed, the only editing I have done is to correct grammar and spelling, and to make the language gender neutral. Second, the sermons are unevenly distributed across the liturgical seasons. For whatever reason, I preached more on Lent—and especially Holy Week—than any other season, on Easter hardly at all, and never on Pentecost. Again, this does not reflect personal taste—especially for one deeply influenced by the Catholic Charismatic Movement—but rather the vagaries of itinerant and occasional preaching.

I have added occasional notes for clarification concerning circumstances, terms, or usages that may seem obscure to some readers.

ADVENT TO CHRISTMAS

THE SEASON OF CRISIS[1]

1 Thessalonians 4:13–18
Matthew 25:1–13

My brothers and sisters in Christ, the cycles of the church's liturgical year are as inexorable as the seasons of nature themselves, and as complex as the cycles of our own lives. In this season of Advent, when we all feel the powers of natural life leeching away with the dying leaves and the fading light—especially those of us whose limbs are fragile and whose sight is frail—in this season, we paradoxically expect the most from God.

Here is the boldness of the Christian imagination, that when our own possibilities are most diminished, we have the highest hope for God's possibilities. And we have precedent.

Which is why, in opposition to the reduction of Advent to the shopping season before Christmas, we join the ancient celebration of Advent as the threefold coming of Jesus: in his birth, in our hearts, and in final triumph.

The scriptural lessons today explicitly focus on that future appearance. They challenge us to revivify the conviction that—with whatever little enthusiasm and with whatever small comprehension—we still declare together when we state, "He will come again in glory to judge the living and the dead."[2]

There are reasons why we lack enthusiasm for so explicit a future eschatology. Most obviously, it is held by all the wrong kind of Christians. We hate to be associated with people whose idea of a happy future is a reclaimed Jerusalem and a scorched earth.

---

1. Cannon Chapel in the Candler School of Theology, Emory University, undated, probably in the 1990s.
2. The Nicene-Constantinopolitan Creed.

And, it has been, after all, a long time to wait. We know that a thousand years are but a moment in God's eyes and so forth (2 Pet 3:8). Still, it's hard to concentrate on a final exam that keeps getting postponed. And then, there is the business of conflicting eschatological scenarios, all of which seem to demand a universe constructed differently than the one that enables the internet.

Let's agree that Paul knew little more about what the future looks like than we do. The clearest evidence is the impossibility of constructing a consistent eschatology from the several letters in which he provides scenarios. I tend to side with those who conclude that Paul constructed such visions of the future with an eye toward their hortatory effect. He was less concerned, in other words, with what might happen next than he was with what his readers should do now.

It is highly likely that Jesus didn't know what the future looked like, either. In Mark's Gospel, at least, Jesus declares himself ignorant of the day and hour of God's future triumph (Mark 13:32).

But Paul and Jesus shared a conviction that governed their view of the future and thereby also shaped their perception of the present. They considered that a God who creates the world as good and humans as free, and who has cared enough for this world to address it through prophets, and incorporate God's very Word in its flesh, would not leave this mysterious and fascinating work half done. Because Paul and Jesus were able to imagine the world as one to which God is faithful to the end, they were able to speak in images about realities they could by no means describe.

To comfort the Thessalonian believers who were despairing because their loved ones were dying before Jesus returned, Paul imagined the share that all humans would have in God's final victory through Christ. He offers them, it is true, a complex apocalyptic vision of clouds and trumpets and angels. But his point is simple: they should not grieve over their dead as people do who have no hope. The reason? The same power at work in the resurrection of Jesus, and that now strengthens their own hearts in dispositions of faith and love, also grounds their hope for their loved ones who have died. Unlike the dead idols they used to worship as gentiles, theirs is the Living God!

God creates the world from nothing. God raises Jesus from the dead to more powerful life. God's Spirit transforms their lives. Raising all the dead in the future? Mere dénouement. Can this be demonstrated? No, but

THE SEASON OF CRISIS

it can be imagined, and therefore can be hoped. Here are our hearts. Look, they do not grieve.

Jesus's parable is both simpler and more threatening. The moment of judgment, he suggests, is not something in the far by-and-by, but is something that can happen any day; not in the clouds but on the ground; not in the bright light of divine radiance, but in the shadows of a long and weary night.

We find this parable of the ten virgins in a series of eschatological parables in Matt 24–25, all of them pointing to the return of the Son of Man. As with all of Jesus's parables, we find here the otherness of first-century Palestine culture, and also the nearness of our own human nature. Lots of details in the parable are unclear because they are embedded in the long-ago and far-away that is only partially recoverable. We are simply not sure what the function of virgins lighting the way for the bridegroom might have been. We know even less about where people in those days could get an oil refill at midnight.

Two aspects of this specific parable would have especially delighted those in the early church who told it with reference to the return of Jesus. The first is that the scene of a personage visiting a city and its inhabitants going out in procession to greet that dignitary corresponds exactly to the royal visits that were designated as *Parousia*, whose imagery Paul also employs in 1 Thessalonians.

The second is that the image of greeting a bridegroom recalls not only the ancient trope of the marriage between Yahweh and Israel, but even more specifically, Jesus's own mysterious self-designation as the Bridegroom (Mark 2:19). The early Christians hearing this parable from Matthew's Gospel read to them would not have thought the distance great from this scene to the one at the very end of the book of Revelation: "The Spirit and the Bride say, 'Come . . . Come, Lord Jesus'" (Rev 22:17, 20). Such complex associations help us grasp how the church eventually developed its threefold understanding of Advent.

As so often also with Jesus's parables, the closer we look, the more puzzling the parable itself becomes. It is clear that the end of the parable declares a judgment on those who were the foolish virgins. The door closed on them; they were not let into the bridegroom's wedding feast. The bridegroom personally and harshly dismisses them: "I do not know you."

Was tardiness then so great an offense in Mediterranean culture? Further, why are some of these virgins "foolish" and others "prudent" or

5

"wise"? The terms echo themes in Matthew's Gospel—the wise are those building their house on rock rather than on sand (7:24), and, immediately before this story, Jesus speaks of the wise household servant whom the master finds at his duties when he arrives (24:45). Notice that the virgins are named as foolish or wise, not at the end, but in the very beginning. And there is surely a connection between their foolishness and the ultimate exclusion from the feast. The judgment, we suppose, is one they have brought on themselves.

But how were they "foolish"? Here is where it gets murky, for unless we are to think of foolishness as a metaphysical condition, the parable must want us to see their foolishness in their actions. It's not as though only five fell asleep while others stayed watching. They all fell asleep. And the wise virgins are not exactly models of solidarity, are they? "Go get your own oil," they say, "we need all we have for ourselves." So this is clearly not a lesson about sharing possessions. And why did the virgins need lamps, anyway? Surely the people in the procession had their own, or they would not have been able to arrive. They did not need any of the virgins' lamps to find their way through the gate.

The most obvious way in which five of the virgins were foolish is that they forgot to bring a reserve of oil for their lamps in case the bridegroom was delayed. So, they were unprepared. A good lesson for boy scouts and obsessive-compulsives. Always be prepared for anything. Wear belt and suspenders. Bring an extra sweater. Carry an extra gallon of oil.

But the parable does not really make clear that *any* of the virgins needed to have their lamps burning in order to meet the bridegroom. But apparently, they thought they did. Here, I think, may be where the real moment of foolishness and the real point of the parable might be found. Just as I have allowed these intricate details make me so obsessive that I almost missed the most obvious thing, so, I think, did the virgins worry so much about having a lit lamp that they missed the procession altogether. And thus, they were foolish.

They are a bit like our friends who are so preoccupied with getting the right picture that they always manage to be looking at their cameras when the planes fly overhead, or the child catches a balloon, or a parade passes by. The point of having the virgins waiting for the bridegroom, it seems, was to honor the bridegroom by having a crowd to greet him. It was not how bright their lamps made the night.

THE SEASON OF CRISIS

They were foolish because they mistook the accidental for the essential. Their job was to be there. In order to be prepared in the manner everyone else was, they risked missing the bridegroom altogether. And they guessed wrong. The bridegroom, it appears, is not in the least bit concerned about their lamps, for when they do show up with their lamps all bright—they had apparently found an all-night oil shop after all—he still dismisses them. They had not been among the greeters—his people—when he came. He does not know them. They could be trick-or-treaters from another neighborhood.

By imagining the time of crisis as something future, or as something happening to others, Paul and Jesus shape in their hearers an ability to imagine the crisis as present and as happening to them. This is what the church learned from these accounts, and led it to think of Advent in terms of a threefold coming. For, in the strictest sense, Christians in every age of the church are no closer to the final triumph of God in the world than were the first believers, and believers in every age of the church are also no further away from the start of that triumph in the birth, life, death, and resurrection of Jesus, than were the first Christians.

To state this is not to deny our own historical character, but to affirm it of ourselves rather than God. We may be closer to the end and farther from the beginning, but God is not, God's triumph in the world is not only future but present. God's judgment of us is not only future, but now. Every day is God's today.

Every day our hope in the power of God demonstrated by the resurrection asks to be translated into hearts that do not grieve and lives that are, as Paul says, sober and watchful as are those of daytime people. Every night our expectation of God's call to us asks that we do not confuse our good performance with God's perfect plan, but that, wickless or wicked, well-fueled or depleted, enlightened or clueless, we have the good sense to stand in the right place.

THE COMING OF THE LORD[1]

Isaiah 55:1–13
James 5:7–11

My sisters and brothers in Christ, Advent is the time of the year when we celebrate, memorialize, pay attention to, and symbolize, waiting for the coming of the Lord.

It is an altogether seductive season. We have the chance to read all the glorious, resonant prophetic texts, and romantically project ourselves back into what we fantasize was the expectation of Israel for its Messiah, and thus liturgically replay the Bible story, and come to Christmas with something more satisfying to the heart than Muzak and mistletoe. As far as games go, this is not a bad one.

Or we can, like Bernard of Clairvaux, celebrate Advent as the coming of the Lord into our hearts through grace. This too, though a bit private, is nice.

Or we can, knowing full well that the New Testament itself speaks about a further coming of the Lord, a return of the Messiah in glory, and knowing full well that this so ardently awaited coming has never (so far as we know) taken place, and knowing how embarrassing it would be for sophisticated Christians like us to be caught, like Garner Ted Armstrong,[2] with our eschatology showing, we can do a theological spin and dip; we can translate the coming of the Lord as the Future that Approaches Us and provides the Ground of our Hope, or some such thing. And this too, although a bit more confusing, is not altogether a bad game.

But the plain truth is, we have heard too much about comings of various sorts, fulfilled and unfulfilled, and are all too confused by different sorts of expectations, frustrated and fruitful: waiting for Godot, waiting for Lefty,

1. Marquand Chapel, Yale Divinity School, 1976.
2. A popular televangelist of the period.

waiting for the washing cycle to end, waiting for Amtrak, waiting for the Lord.

So, we figure it is not totally a bad thing for Christmas to come and relieve us of all our temporal tension, all this three-layered going and coming, and we can rest again in the sweet memory of the past, and shelve until the next Advent wreath the complexities of eschatology.

Now, I don't know what to make of all this, either. I don't really see how we can speak of God "coming" and "going" in the first place. How can we talk about the Mystery whose heartbeat is the pulse of creation, or, to be less medical, Whose presence is at once affirmed in this space by the fact that all of us are breathing, and Whose absence is affirmed by the fact that it is only we who seem to be breathing, how can we talk about This One, blessed be the Name, coming and going?

Does God, then, come and go, ebb and flow?

Or can we reduce it to a matter of perception, to a matter of "theological anthropology," to a matter of changing attitudes, thusly: If we *think* He is coming, then, for us, God is coming. Oh dear.

It is a bit offensive, it is more than a little harsh, when we hear Isaiah tell us that every word that God has spoken will return to him fulfilled, and then turn to James and see the good moralist, this sacred writer, flogging the rich who oppress the poor and telling them, you just wait, you wait till the Lord comes, you'll get yours, and then hear him telling the ones being oppressed—the ones he is talking to—that they should be patient, for the Lord is coming, with the clear implication, again, that they will get their reward, as the rich will get their punishment... It shakes us, as we listen to these sacred words together as we have just come from the streets of Muzak and mistletoe, hearing, "He's making a list, he's checking it twice, he's going to find out who's naughty or nice," and not being able *not* to make the connection.

Only, even little brats don't really get switches and ashes, and everyone gets something good from that jolly voyeur who sees them when they're sleeping and knows when they're awake.

But those poor and oppressed people James was speaking to—did their patience do them any good? Did the "establishment of their hearts"? Did the Lord come for them? Did they know when he came? Did it make a difference? And just as pertinently, those rich oppressors, did they get punished?

And the millions of Jews in the Holocaust, who *knew* that the Messiah was surely coming because their suffering was so unthinkably great, did he come for them?

Perhaps we slip into nostalgia and pretty theologizing about the past at Christmas, because the terrible promise of his coming remains unfulfilled, and we don't know how to handle that.

This has nothing to do with our being touched by the life of the risen Lord, yes, Lord, and thank you. It has nothing to do with the Future as the Ground of our Hope, yes, Lord, and thank you.

But Lord: when will you come in a way that the rich and the poor, the oppressors and the oppressed, can tell the difference?

So we thank you, Lord, for giving us patience, because without it, we don't know what we would do; for establishing our hearts, because without such simplicity and strength of longing, we know we would be utterly lost in Muzak and mistletoe.

So we thank you, Lord, for coming to us in the ways that we can, sneakily and by a sideways glance, perceive, as in your Word, today, and in your silent acceptance of us.

And we thank you, Lord, Blessed God, for keeping the mystery of your coming safely beyond the reach of our cleverness.

And having thanked you for all these blessings, we ask you Lord, to come in a way that makes a difference.

HOPE AND COMMITMENT[1]

Genesis 28:10–21
Romans 8:18–26

My brothers and sisters in Christ, when I was in high school, I acted in a play of mildly existentialist pretensions called *Hope Is the Thing with Feathers*.[2] The title caused much discussion among us would-be thespians and theologians. Was the author pointing to the elusiveness of hope, fleeing like a bird from our grasp? Or was he making an allusion to the Holy Spirit? The play itself did not make clear, and, in fact, was not as good as its title, which belonged to Emily Dickinson in the first place. And I am not much further along in my understanding of the matter.

I used to think that hope was what enabled commitment. I could leap because there was something (I was sure) to catch me on the other side. Hope had to do with the future. It was the world of my possibilities. And since in those days of energy and exuberance such possibilities seemed infinite, so was my hope. So also seemed my ability to commit myself. But to what? Now, I suspect, myself, in my imagined future.

So I see young Jacob on his journey to get a wife. He had not before this dealt much in divinity. But he slept beside the sacred pillar and dreamed of angels in the night sky. He heard the ancient promise of his father Isaac and the old man Abraham before him. God said, "Behold, I am with you, and will keep you wherever you go." And he said, further, "I will bring you back to this land."

This was the part Jacob really heard because it coincided with his own view of his future exactly, and what else is God for, if not to confirm our desires? Jacob knew the gate of heaven when he saw it, and leaped, and said,

1. Marquand Chapel, Yale Divinity School, 1981.
2. The play was written by Richard Harrity and played on Broadway in 1948; he took the title, of course, from Emily Dickinson.

"If God is with me . . . and gives me bread to eat (a new codicil) . . . then the Lord will be my God." Jacob committed himself to his own future, the future secured his hope. He could leap, if only conditionally.

But the next time Jacob met his Lord (Gen 32:22–32), he learned what "I am with you" means when it is God who speaks. Again, it was night. Now, however, no bright visions. Only the sweaty, deadly wrestling with an assassin in the dark. Jacob in agony held on, held on until dawn, screaming at the pain in his thigh. He won a bitter victory. He gained a new name, and he walked ever after with a limp. "I have seen God face to face," he declared, "and have lived." This he called a blessing when he told his children the story and warned them about the hip bone.

Where were Jacob's conditions now? And where was his hope? Jacob had to reconsider, as do we all who ever get past the stage of infatuation with heavenly dreams. Now he learned that the point was not his commitment to his own future, or even his commitment to Yahweh. The point was rather than Yahweh was committed to him.

And if Yahweh was one to creep into his tent at night and do such vicious battle, then all bets were off for a predictable future. This Holy One struck like lightning. So, what of Jacob's hope? It was found in that searing pain of God's visitation.

It was not because of hope that he could commit himself to God. It was because God had committed himself to Jacob that this bewildered cripple could hope. Jacob learned about hope that it is not a view of the future but a perception of the present.

Which is somewhat like Paul's bold paradox. Here is all this pain, Paul says, all this travail. The whole world is like one great labor contraction. Hear the scream? Well, let's call it hope. Why? Because we recognize the grace in the pain. We know the touch of this visitor from the ancient ache in our bones from long ago in our story. Both the angel and the Spirit cry out for freedom.

If commitment is another name for the mystery of freedom, if hope is another name for that inexplicable thing that enables us to keep walking instead of stopping, then we are in the realm of gift and not of achievement. We do better to ponder than to preach such hard realities.

We who have learned much in these years of despondency and despair, depression and slow death, know how hollow are the words of easy hope. We who have known the one who declares, as she cries out that she cannot

HOPE AND COMMITMENT

get through even this day, cannot even get out of bed, "there is nothing to hope for," know as well how right she is, and how unable we are to help.

We could state, of course, the obvious connection between her inability to act—that is, her inability to choose, commit herself—and her lack of hope. But she knows it already, better than we do. And our learned analysis does not help. We sense with her that whatever we know of hope we learn together in the touch of our hands, here and now. As we have learned from our God, it is out of painful commitment one to the other that hope grows.

Some of us in this place, some of us in this room, do not know whether we can make it through this day. Literally. We do not feel, sense, anything to hope in, anything that will help us put one foot in front of the other. What all of us should know with our minds, namely that we die every minute, some of us are feeling in our hearts, and we grow paralyzed with fear. There are no easy words to cover this.

The gift is not ours to give. But we should acknowledge to each other, at least, what we scarcely wish to acknowledge even to ourselves. Those of us who still walk, or even run, do so by a gift we cannot account for and cannot control. We also do not know when we shall hit the wall and stop. We do not know how much of our hopefulness is high spirits and the wash of enzymes.

So those of us who walk and those of us who wait can only, as we reach out to touch one another, learn of hope from the pain, and give thanks, guardedly. As those do who, while obviously dying, say they are giving birth.

CHRISTMAS PRESENT[1]

Ephesians 2:1–10
Luke 3:1–3

My brothers and sisters in Christ, through all the centuries of retelling and reimagining, in words, and music, and art, the Christmas story has become softened for us, almost other-worldly. Perhaps the dominant emotion aroused in us when we hear its familiar cadences is a sort of diffuse nostalgia . . . for what? For our own lost innocence, for our childhood? Or perhaps, for the childhood of the world (we think), when there *were* real shepherds and wise men and when angels seemed plausible and comforting entities.

Nostalgia is not altogether bad, but it can distort. It can confuse for us the real meaning of God's coming into our world as one of us. The danger is that the story becomes a sort of fairy tale, which, like all fairy tales has charm, but also has little contact with the harsh truths of life.

The Gospels are much less sentimental. If we read them with care, and try to cut through the levels of sweetness with which we have coated them, we discover that the world into which Jesus was born looked disturbingly, frighteningly, like our own.

In today's gospel passage, St. Luke sets the scene for the beginning of John the Baptist's preaching in the desert. To show that this took place in a real time and place, he gives a list of the world rulers when John's ministry began.

It is quite a list. From the ruthlessly efficient but exotically perverse Tiberius Caesar, who ruled from his villa in Capri over the vast and ruthlessly efficient Roman empire, to the corrupt high priests Annas and Caiphas, toadies to the rich and traitors to their own people, the list stinks with

---

1. Fourth Sunday of Advent, 1969, preached to monastic community of St. Joseph Abbey and congregation.

corruption. And if we go behind these great figures and read between the lines of the Gospels, we discover the world of first-century Palestine to be fully as confused, bitter, and angry as our own.

It was a land occupied by a hated foreign invader, with the vast majority of the people overtaxed and underfed, while a select few gorged on the rewards of oppression and graft. It was a land split between rich and poor, and split again into multiple factions representing political and religious rivalries, split by hate for each other and united only by a shared detestation of Rome. It was a land in which young men became armed resistance fighters, and where some of them roamed the streets of Jerusalem as professional assassins. It was a land in which ten thousand executions at one time was not unheard of.

This is the world to which John preached. And it killed him. This is the world into which God's Son became human and lived among humans. And it was this world that crucified Jesus. It is *our* world.

When we look around us today and see, not the joy and peace and love proclaimed by Hallmark cards, but the same war and oppression, the same corruption in high places and apathy in low places, the same bitterness and hatred and dissension (even within ourselves), we are tempted to ask: what has changed? Has the coming of Jesus made any real difference in the world? Is Christmas, after all, only the symbolic representation of a futile ideal? Is it a false vision of a never-existing sweetness and light that lets us escape, however briefly, the burden of our own reality?

My sisters and brothers, if we can face that question in all its clarity and pain, we are in a much better position for understanding what Christmas is, not as a story about the past but as a truth about the present.

We are then perhaps ready to realize what it actually means for truth to enter a world of falsehood, for love to come into a world of hate.

We may begin to see that the love of God can only establish itself in this world of ours through suffering the death imposed by the world. We begin to see that the death of Jesus is not an accident—as though the wonderful promise of his nativity had somehow been cancelled—but that the death of Jesus is the logical termination of the process of suffering through which God showed his absolute love for and to the world.

Perhaps then we will be ready to grasp that the kingdom of love and peace that Jesus truly did establish in his blood on the cross does not drop down out of heaven fully accomplished, requiring of us only that we admire and sign on. The kingdom of God becomes a reality for us only when each truly appropriates for himself or herself the saving death of Jesus. And this is done in only one way: by following the same path of self-emptying love even to death for our brothers and sisters.

Christmas is not just in the past; it is a moveable feast. The birth of the Word of God into the world happens every time people open themselves to the power of God and let God's power gain entry, not just to the compartment of their brain marked Sunday, but into every nook and cranny of their lives, into their real world of work and business and politics and family and play.

If this year our celebration of Jesus's birth is not accompanied by such a personal appropriation of his life; if Christ is not born anew in our hearts and in our lives this Christmas, then the answer to our question must be, "No, the coming of Jesus as not really made any difference in *our* world," and thus, our celebration of his birth is only an exercise in fantasy.

But if we allow him to be born again in our lives, then we can with joy look forward to that "Christmas Future" which is his final and glorious coming, even as we now with joy remember his coming first in the flesh, and even as we now greet him and each other this morning in breaking the bread of thanksgiving.

THE MYSTERY THAT IS CHRISTMAS[1]

Like many who quietly teach the New Testament, I am accustomed to being ignored by the press in every season of the year except Easter and Christmas. In these two seasons, I must field the inevitable questions from local reporters, "What's new on the resurrection?" or, "Anything new on Christmas?"

What the media seeks is something novel and perhaps titillating that has been uncovered by historical research, preferably something that calls into question the miracle of Jesus's conception and birth, or the wonder of Jesus's death and resurrection. My answer never varies: "The same thing is new now as when Jesus was born and when Jesus was raised," I say, "and that is good news from God." Small wonder that I get fewer such calls each year.

Newspapers are sold, after all, because of their ability to provide novel variations on the same old themes of a tired world: envy, exploitation, rivalry, oppression, competition, violence, exclusion, murder. The news media specializes in identifying problems and revealing secrets. But newscasts and newspapers do not comprehend mystery.

Indeed, most of us who are readers of newspapers and watchers of computer and television screens have lost the sense of mystery as well. Even those seeking to be religious find themselves coopted by the universal pragmatism of commerce, seduced by the shiny surfaces of efficiency and profit. Even they find it hard to resist the message of every jingle, every ad, that Christmas is about going to the mall.

Christmas is not, however, about maintaining the national economy or meeting societal expectations. It is about a mystery so large and yet so quiet that even when it has been revealed it cannot be comprehended.

---

1. This reflection—which is very much like a homily—was composed around 2000 for Beliefnet.

ADVENT TO CHRISTMAS

The mystery is simply that God enters humanity and makes it new. The gift-giving that defines Christmas is this exchange whereby God and humans embrace.

Here the language of history is totally inadequate, for all history is able to do is record the surface of human events. For the mystery that is Christmas, the language of myth is needed. Only the language of myth is able to express what lies beneath the surface of things, yet is most true.

The language of history is like the language of the news media. It can only express variations on surface sameness. But the language of myth can sing the sweet song of transformation deep down things. Christians who have not entirely lost their wits appreciate that the Christmas story as told in the Gospels of Matthew and Luke is true precisely because it is mythic. If the Christmas story were simply a historical report, then it could also be only about human experiences. Such experiences or events might be interesting, even charming. But they would not matter to all other humans in all times and places. Only if God is at work in these events and experiences do they matter to everyone, and to speak of God, one must use other than historical language.

To speak the inexpressible truth that God embraces humanity by becoming a specific human being in Jesus, even mythic language strains the limits of paradox: a virgin conceives and gives birth; the night becomes as bright as day; shepherds from their fields and magicians from a far country gather in silent awe as the creator of the universe becomes small in a child. God embraces humanity not in King Herod, but in the shepherd David's lowliest descendent, not in merchants and entrepreneurs who run the country, but in the poor and despised who dwell in the land.

God chose to renew the world not through armies or politics or commerce, but by living the simplest of human lives, beginning with the most elemental of all human experiences, the birth of a baby. God's interest is not in political rearrangements but in the transformation of human existence. God's power is revealed not in King Herod's ability to slaughter little children, but in the Virgin Mary's care to caress and comfort her child.

So, I am reminded each year that if I want to see signs of God's renewal of the world, I should not seek them by scanning headlines or surfing channels.

I should learn again to stop, and to be silent. I should learn to wait for surface distractions to cease, at least for a moment, so that I might enter a depth that most of my busyness serves to deny.

By becoming silent and still, I might notice again the way a tiny baby grasps its father's finger and gazes at its mother's face. And when I learn to see again that way—perceiving what is real rather than what is apparent—I might again be able to tell the difference between secrets and mysteries, between change and transformation, between the same old gossip and the ever-new good news.

SHAPED BY THE WORD[1]

Romans 10:1–13
Luke 2:15–20

My brothers in Christ, what the shepherds ran to see was the king of Israel, a savior for all the people. What they saw was the most ordinary of sights: the poor baby of a poor and transient couple. There was a great difference between the words that had been spoken to them from heaven, and their actual experience. But they nevertheless went back rejoicing, believing that this child was the king.

They believed, not alone because of their experience, but because of the word that had been spoken over that experience, the word of God that shaped it and gave it a meaning that was not obvious to human sight. Their experience alone could not have convinced them. For when Jesus came, he did not come palpably as God, in manifest power, in evident divinity. He came as dew on the grass, quietly, ordinarily, insignificantly. He was born as all men are born, of a woman. And as a Jew, he was born as were all his fellow Jews, under the law.

It was the word of good news, the gospel, that enabled the shepherds to see and believe the deeper dimensions of this ordinary birth. Their faith came, as all faith must come, from hearing, from hearing the word of God that establishes and interprets all that is real, establishes *by* interpreting what is real in human experience, even in (or especially in) the face of the evidence of their senses, and their belief transformed their experience, and they rejoiced.

The shepherds spoke to Mary of what they had been told. And from their words, she too was given faith. Mary's faith also came from hearing. She heard, and turned the words over in her heart, and believed. Although her experience was apparently ordinary and common, the words she heard

1. Preached to the monastic community, St. Joseph Abbey, 1969.

led her to believe in the uncommon and extraordinary significance of that experience.

Our lives here also appear to be the most ordinary and humdrum of lives. We grope and struggle. We are a blind striving-after. We act and interact in the obscurity of our own weakness and sin. Our experience alone cannot convince us of the significance of who we are and what we are doing. It is the word of God spoken over our lives that convinces us. The word of God leads us to understand the extraordinary fact that this very life of ambiguity is the sign and realization of God's saving presence in the world, that we are graced.

This may seem to be saying too much, but only if we insist on regarding the word as somehow exterior to experience. It is not. Word is internal to experience and makes it what it is. We can see this even in our own lives. If someone I trust and love assures me that another person, whom I only vaguely know, is untrustworthy or wicked, that word shapes my experience of the person. That person is, so far as I am concerned, untrustworthy and wicked. My perception of an attitude toward that person is inevitably affected by interpretation; I respond to him distrustfully. But if I am told that this person is trustworthy and loving, then my approach to him is open and trusting. The word not only interprets. By interpreting, it transforms.

If this is so for our frail and feeble human speech, how much more is it the case for the all-powerful word of God?

For us as for the shepherds, the Word comes to us where we live, the extraordinary within the ordinary, as simply as the birth of a child that is the incarnation of God's Son. It comes to us in the humble words of the sacred texts, in the words of fellowship and celebration over bread and wine, and through the loving words of our brothers, not only in instruction and correction, but also in the incarnate words of assistance and sharing and affection and forgiveness of faults.

If we, like Mary, can open our hearts to such words, and can ponder them in the quiet prayer that is our simple presence before God and our own existence—which in its ultimate depths *is* presence before God—then we too can be brought to deeper faith, so that the Word can transform our experience itself from sinful bondage to the liberty of grace.

And the Word is this, that it is precisely here in our shared experience that we find the Word, the Living Word. We do not need to scale heaven, or to descend to the depths of the earth. The Word is very near to us. It is on our lips and in our hearts, when we confess that Jesus is our Lord, and believe in our hearts that God has raised him from the dead. This we confess and believe in the action we are about to share.

LENT

FASTING AND DIETING[1]

Isaiah 58:1–12
Matthew 6:1–16

My sisters and brothers in Christ, the prophet Isaiah and Jesus had mixed feelings about fasting. We do too. In this, we are like Jesus and the prophet Isaiah. Of course, we have different reasons. Jesus and the prophet Isaiah liked fasting because they saw it as an attempt by people to draw near to God. The prophet Isaiah and Jesus disliked fasting because it could so easily become a way of manipulating God.

We, on the other hand, like fasting for what it does to our waistline, but we hate what it does to our temper. We like what it does for our self-esteem (such discipline), but we hate what it does to our nerves. On the whole, then, we like dieting much better.

Dieting takes care of our waistline and self-esteem and does not fray our nerves and make us act abruptly in company.

Jesus and the prophet left no record of their opinion on dieting.

Maybe that is because in their world, people did not diet. People feasted, and people fasted, but, so far as we know, people did not diet. For one thing, there was not as much food around then, as now. People diet when there is too much food generally, and when there is certainly too much food getting into peoples' mouths.

When there is not so much food around, one can see what there is as gift, and celebrate by feasting. This is appropriate. When there is not so much food, one can see more clearly how close death is, perhaps the lack of a bite away.

It comes down, finally, as it always does, to how we see death and life.

When life is seen as a gift, feasting is an act of thanksgiving. When death is seen as the sign that this life is but a step on the way, it is a good

1. Ash Wednesday, Trinity Church on the Green, New Haven, Connecticut, 1979.

idea to fast, for fasting is a form of dying and it reminds us of the real thing, a real thing not so far future but happening to each one of us now, since we are, each one of us, dying even now as we live.

Now here is a subtle point. Dieting is a way of avoiding death. Yes, it is. We diet and jog and watch obscure grams and carbohydrates because we want to feel good, look good, look young, and not like people who are dying. People who seriously fast look like they are dying and feel like they are dying. It is awful.

Fasting is a reminder of death, that is, a reminder of the truth.

We need a reminder like that, from time to time. We need such a reminder, because, left to ourselves, we would probably diet, and live much longer and look much better and forget that we are lying to ourselves and to God. To ourselves and to God. Of course, God is not fooled. But we may be. And it is, after all, our life and our death, the only one we have.

But Jesus and the prophet Isaiah worried about fasting, too, and rightly, for fasting also can contain a lie, all the more destructive for being so close to the truth.

Fasting can be a kind of narcissism, a self-involvement more subtle and more insidious for being more spiritual. A person can fast, thinking, "This obligates God; look, God what I have done for you. You owe me."

Or, as Jesus points out, a person can fast to win a reputation, a reputation for being ascetical, spiritual. Giving up a little, gaining a lot.

So, Jesus and the prophet Isaiah say, "Fast by all means, but let your fasting be an expression of faith." How can fasting be an expression of faith? When it is a mode of praying and when it is a mode of almsgiving.

When we pray truly, we do not manipulate God, but wait quietly upon him, listening for his voice, attentive to the whisper of his will in the structure of our lives. We place our lives in his hands, from which they have come as a gift, and say, "Not my will be done, but yours."

How does fasting help us pray in this way? Because when we are genuinely hungry and try to pray, we learn how insistent and demanding are all the other voices in our heads, all the voices around and within us, the voices of craving and desire. Fasting does not take them away. No. It simply reminds us of what is there all the time. It reminds us of just how much we need the prayer of quiet. It reminds us that if we are to say "yes" to God in the moments of our life, then we must also die to those voices that clamor within us, saying, "Eat, possess, rule, gain, grab."

FASTING AND DIETING

And when we give alms, that is, when we place our possessions at the disposal of others in need—and others are always in need of what we possess (not only money but time, and energy, and space, and care, above all care)—then we are in fact listening to the voice of God in our lives and obeying his call, which is faith.

How does fasting help us give alms in this way?

Because when we are genuinely hungry and not just dieting, we are reminded of how tightly we cling to every crust, every moment, every idea, every inch of our space, and just how much dying we must do if we are to move into God's life.

Fasting is not some work we accomplish that takes away the need for grace. Just the opposite. Fasting is allowing our need for grace to become manifest in our flesh.

As it was in the flesh of Jesus, the pioneer and perfecter of our faith, who, in learning obedience by what he suffered, opened once for all our own capacity to move toward God in faithful obedience, becoming progressively with each yes, perfect Son; stepping out of our partial truth into the boundless truth of God's love, dying to our self-preoccupation, to live in his will.

And in this, the Christian Lenten fast leads to Easter, just as the death which is ingredient to faith leads to a share in the glorious resurrection; both suffering and glory, both fasting and feasting; a celebration of God's Spirit at play in our hearts.

THE OLD AND NEW ADAM[1]

Genesis 3:1–6
Romans 5:12–20
Matthew 4:1–11

My sisters and brothers in Christ, the church's calendar tells time differently than does MTV or Hallmark. The church tells time by the liturgy: each year in their worship, Christians retrace the seasons of redemption. MTV and Hallmark tell time by the clock of commerce. They have room for Santa and the Easter Bunny, but not for the Cross and Resurrection. While Hallmark has reminded us for weeks of Valentine's Day, it sells no greeting card for Lent.

Yet, by the church's calendar, that's where we are today, in the first Sunday of Lent. Today, we hand ourselves over—not always willingly, not always gladly—to the ritual progression of the church's most ancient liturgical cycle. In worship, we move day by day to Lent and Easter. In our lives, we seek to move with Jesus through the days of his ministry and suffering, so that we arrive at Easter as *Christians*. As Paul says in his Letter to the Philippians, "We do this so that we might know him and the power of his resurrection, and may share in his sufferings, becoming like him in death that if possible we may attain the resurrection from the dead" (Phil 3:10–11).

We do not submit to Lent gladly, because we are, all of us, captive to the glitter and glamour of the worlds of commerce and advertising, the noise of celebrity, and the lures of random pleasures. But despite all the clamor outside us and all the noise within us, we dedicate ourselves, for this season, to imagining the world differently than do MTV, Hallmark, and the other instruments of contemporary seduction. We allow ourselves

---

1. Oak Grove Presbyterian Church, Bloomington, Minnesota, 2008.

to be shaped by these simple, yet powerful stories. We take on the church's ancient disciplines of prayer and fasting and almsgiving.

These disciplines are not a form of self-improvement—fasting is not dieting. They are not a way of concentrating our attention—Lent is not Ramadan. They are not an exercise in masochism—what I gave up for Lent.

They are, instead, ways of unmasking the hard truth of our existence that so much of our daily distraction, daily pleasure, daily chores, serve to camouflage.

Nothing so exposes the truth of our lives as sitting in silence and hearing the noise within our heads, or staying hungry until our irritation reminds us how insatiable and promiscuous are our appetites, or sharing our possessions until we feel that something essential to us has been lost, learning thereby how consistently we identify our being with our having.

When we are schooled by such disciplines, however, we are also better able to be shaped by the stories we have heard this morning. They too speak to the truth of our condition. They locate the mystery of our freedom between the burden we inherit from our parents (Adam and Eve) and the gift we have been given by our brother (Jesus). They locate the place of decision between the influence of Adam and Christ. They identify our choice as one between sin and faith.

It is always humbling to realize that the great drama of sin and faith cannot be played out simply in our heads. It must always from beginning to end engage our inescapable, intractable, indecipherable bodies. From the garden planted for our parents to the desert sought by our brother to the tables around which we gather, the drama of sin and faith in enacted by the most elemental of physical things, the disposition, action, and suffering of our bodies. And how our bodies dispose of this apple, those stones, that bread, this cherry pie, that piece of clothing, this embrace, these tears.

Now around such simple physical elements we do indeed spin the most elaborate mental webs of fantasy and desire, of rationalization and self-delusion: "She saw that the tree was good for food, and that it was a delight to the eyes, and that the tree was to be desired to make one wise" (Gen 3:6). Beauty, pleasure, utility: the classic variations on the idolatrous impulse to center on the gift rather than the giver, to usurp, indeed, the role of the giver: "I can give him fruit that not even God will let him have." It is the same in the desert as in the garden: "These stones become bread can prove my power, this leap from a deadly height can coerce God's care, this seizure of world rule can subdue what God cannot!"

Simple elements of the body. Complex designs of the mind. So, in the end, the heart must choose whose voice to trust, whose call to obey.

In the garden, with the abundance of God's gifts all around, the subtle serpent seemed a sage in its glib denial of God's decree: "God does not want you to have knowledge, experience of good and evil, God is jealous of your ability to grow. You won't die" (Gen 3:4–5). For beauty, for pleasure, for utility, for the chance to seize for themselves and give to each other what—they could argue—did not come to them from God, our parents ate, and died. Just so, in all the ways we trust delusion and obey deception, do we all die in Adam.

In the desert, where God's gifts seem few and unappealing, where human need is stripped to the bone of hunger and thirst, the tempter's voice is still more insistent: "You are, it seems, God's son. If you are, eat, you will live; if you are, throw yourself down, you will not die; if you are, seize power for yourself that does not come from God. You will not fail!" (Matt 4:3, 6, 9).

But our brother Jesus was schooled in the discipline of prayer and fasting; he was shaped by the stories and songs of the people God had so patiently prepared in the long years outside the garden in other deserts, and he was ready for the test. In his heart, Jesus trusted not the suave words of deception and delusion, but the words of the one who gave him his life as a gift and renewed that gift every morning. In his heart, he obeyed the call that is implicit in the gift, the call to be, simply, a human person centered in the giver rather than the gift.

So Jesus answered, using the very words of those stories and songs taught by God, "Not by bread alone do humans live, but by every word from the mouth of God," and, "You shall not tempt the Lord your God," and, "You shall worship the Lord your God; him alone shall you serve" (Matt 4:4, 7, 10).

By so trusting and by so obeying, Jesus opened for us a new possibility of responding to God and God's creation. Paul states it clearly in Romans: "As one human's trespass led to condemnation for all humans, so one human's act of righteousness leads to acquittal and life for all humans. For as by one human's disobedience many were made sinners, so by one human's obedience, many will be established in righteousness" (5:18–19).

During this season of Lent, then, we fast, we pray, we share our possessions, and we pay the strictest attention to these stories, hoping that as they shape our response, empower the decision of our hearts toward the God who gifts us so generously, we also may be shaped in the image of the one who shows us the way of faith. And knowing the end of such schooling to be fuller life here and eternal life hereafter, we can sing with the psalmist, "Steadfast love surrounds the one who trusts in the Lord. Be glad in the Lord and rejoice O you righteous. Shout for joy all you upright in heart" (Ps 32:11).

LIGHT AND LIFE[1]

Ephesians 5:8–14
John 9:1–40

When I am asked to speak to a group of Christians I have not known before—as I have been invited to speak to you this morning—I always base my sermon on the readings provided by the church's lectionary. The reason is that if I pick a text, I am too likely to choose something I like to talk about or think you ought to hear. But since I don't know you, I have no idea what you should hear. And picking a text I like to talk about only ensures that you hear my thoughts and not the word of God.

The lectionary puts a little distance between this preacher and his arrogance and demands that I pay attention to the words we hear together, instead of picking the words of Scripture that agree with what I have already decided to say.

The lectionary also joins all of us in this sanctuary today, even though we do not know each other, in the common story of Christians in every sanctuary on this Sunday. This is a good antidote to our chronic self-preoccupation.

When we hear these readings from Ephesians and from the Gospel of John, we hear and think about words that Christians all over the world hear and think about this morning. I am pulled into a larger world than the one I inhabit when I read the Bible all by myself. And we as a congregation are drawn into a larger Christian consciousness than the one we have when we equate church simply with what is happening here at Second Presbyterian in Roanoke.

In fact, the lectionary also connects us with all the Christians who went before us, who have heard and thought about the Gospel of John and Paul's Letter to the Ephesians. They read and thought about them in

1. Second Presbyterian Church, Roanoke, Virginia, 2005.

particular as they passed through the season of the liturgical year called Lent, the season we also are now passing through.

During the long time of preparation for Easter called Lent, two kinds of processes went on simultaneously. This was when the early church prepared those who were joining the church, the catechumens, for their baptism at the Easter vigil. The lectionary readings were carefully chosen for their instruction. At the same time, those already baptized heard and thought about these texts as part of their Lenten preparation for Easter and enabled them to consider their own state of conversion, how well they actually were living by their own baptismal promises.

This is the first thing I ask you to consider with me this morning, how densely layered our Christian life is. We are linked to all the faithful in the world today, and we are joined to all the saints who have been faithful before us. This makes us different in our culture, which glorifies fleeting celebrity and praises the new and novel and has calibrated attention span to an MTV nanosecond.

Christians are countercultural because they embrace a universal vision of God's people larger than our family and even our nation, because they rejoice in having a history longer and more complex than the memory log of internet usage.

Imagine: when we sing, "Holy, Holy, Holy," we say words first spoken 2,800 years ago. And when we say, "Lord, have mercy," we speak with the words of first-century Palestinian beggars. And when we say, "Our Father," we pray with the words given us by Jesus. How can we not be in awe of this fragile gift of faith that has passed through so many lives like light through the darkness, now to illumine our lives as well?

The second thing I want to think about with you is the way this layering was much the same for the very first believers as it is for us. Think about the way the New Testament compositions were composed. They were written by people like us who had been touched by the Holy Spirit that came from the risen Jesus, and who lived in communities of faith with as diverse and unlikely collection of people as the ones who form Second Presbyterian in Roanoke, Virginia.

When Paul wrote to the Ephesians, he wrote to people who had experienced baptism, and had heard said to them as they rose from the water, "Sleeper, awake! Rise from the dead and Christ will shine on you." For Paul and his readers, Jesus was not a figure of the past, but a living presence shining like light in their lives. When Paul instructs them on how to live according to the light, then, he quotes these baptismal words to them, words from the tradition in order to help them understand how the light that gave them life must also be the light that guided their living together in the world.

The Gospel of John similarly, which announces Jesus in its first lines as the life which was the light of all people, tells the story of Jesus in light of the continuing experience of that life and light in the community. The Gospel of John is not a simple telling of facts about the past. Instead, the story of Jesus is thickly overlaid with the story of the community within which the risen Jesus continued to shine brightly as the light of the world.

The first readers of John's Gospel could therefore read about themselves in the story told about Jesus. They could identify first with the man born blind, for into their lives also Jesus had come as the light and had given them a new vision of reality and the capacity to live in the world with new freedom. But they could also identify with the blind man's parents who were afraid of the authorities because they also had experienced rejection from the synagogue for their confession of Jesus.

Perhaps, though, the first readers of John's Gospel only made this identification: they were in the light and outsiders were in darkness.

But our ancestors in the faith who read this Gospel during Lent, during the time when catechumens were being prepared to receive the light that was Christ, eventually learned to read this Gospel passage at a still more penetrating level. They were able to ask about the ways in which perhaps they resembled the Pharisees in the story more than they did the man who received his sight, or his parents.

They had thought hard about Paul's words to them, how their lives had once been in darkness (like the blind man), and how they were now children of light, and how therefore they must live as children of light. And they had looked at their lives to see whether they lived as people of the light, seeking in everything, as Paul told them, what is good and right and true, that is, what is pleasing to the Lord, and living in such truth, seeking to bring what is darkness into the light.

They considered carefully what it meant not only to receive the light that was Christ, but also to live in the light, and to bring their life and the life of the world into the light.

And having thought hard on those words they began to understand how they sometimes took part in the deeds of darkness, how they also did shameful things in secret that they very much desired not to come to light, how many aspects were in shadow if not in absolute darkness, and how little they did to make light shine more brightly in the world by their seeking in every circumstance what is good, and what is right, and what is true, and what is pleasing to the Lord.

Because they had thought hard on these words during Lent, wondering how they could bring the light of Christ to catechumens if they themselves were so shadowed over, they were more able to see in John's story the resemblance between themselves and the Pharisees, those who refused to see light appear in places they did not expect or had not approved, who when they could not deny that light had shone in the man's eyes tried every means available to deny that the light had come from God.

Why did these deeply religious people work so hard to deny the light shining from the man's eyes even if it required closing their eyes and calling it darkness? Because if they opened their eyes to this new light, then they would have to become children of a light that operated outside of their control or their understanding, they would have to pay closer attention to all the ways in which God's light seeks to give life in the world.

The Lenten Christians who were our ancestors could read the final words of Jesus to the Pharisees, not as addressed to enemies of the light from long ago, but as addressed to them, who had received the light of Christ: "If you were blind, you would not have sin, but now that you say, 'we see,' your sin remains."

So the third and final thing I would ask you to think about this morning and perhaps this Lenten week, is how we can read Scripture in the same layered way our ancestors did, read Ephesians and the Gospel of John not simply as advice and stories from the past and about the past, but God's urgent word addressed to us in our lives.

Can we, perhaps, think together about the ways in which the light that is life has entered our life and transformed it, and be glad? And can we, also, think each one of us about the ways in which we do not altogether live the light, even at times seek to suppress the light?

If we think hard, together and apart, on these things, then we will honor those who have gone before us in the faith and read this way, and will support all those believers throughout the world who listen to these same texts with us today, and will more truly hear the word of God that comes to us this day, will receive the life that is light, and from it learn how to lead lives that give light.

AVARICE THE DEADLY SIN[1]

Romans 2:25–29
John 2:13–21

My brothers and sisters in Christ, we find ourselves this morning in the third Sunday in Lent. And, partway through a series of sermons on the Seven Deadly Sins. Such a series has its advantages and its disadvantages. There is something to be gained by examining the astonishing versatility of our declensions. We find that we can, and do, corrupt every human endeavor. It's not a bad thing, indeed it is remarkably sobering, to contemplate the precise ways we distort our lives, and how, driven by fear and compulsion, we can make any part of God's creation an idol—something that distorts the world and destroys us.

The disadvantage of such a series of sermons is, first, that it places the preacher—especially a guest preacher—in an impossible dilemma. Should I preach on the texts of Scripture for this Sunday, my usual practice—or should I preach on the theme of the Seven Deadly Sins? It is hard enough just to preach the texts, and to bring them into a creative conversation with our lives. But to bend them and our lives to fit a preordained theme? This calls either for a *tour de force* or great luck, neither of which seem available to your preacher today. So, for this once, I will leave the texts aside, unless by chance you see connections that I do not—which would not, in fact, surprise me.

A second disadvantage to such a series on the Seven Deadly Sins is that it might start us thinking about *sins* (in the plural), as though they were discrete and separable acts that could thus be catalogued. Then we could divide our lives into neat compartments; we could avoid some sins while we concentrate on others. I may be envious, but I don't commit gluttony. Or, I eat way too much, but I am not proud. This way of thinking about

---

1. Preached at Saint Mark's Cathedral, Seattle, Washington, 1985.

AVARICE THE DEADLY SIN

sin (or sins) is both common and ancient, going all the way back to the Greek philosophers' analysis of vices and virtues. Such analyses were, in truth, startlingly accurate in their psychological awareness. Aristotle and Plutarch—to take two of the outstanding examples—saw clearly the ways that humans foul their own freedom. They perceived, for example, that if all vice is a sickness of the soul, then surely envy is best considered as an ulcer.

Such study of virtues and vices, however, had as its horizon only relations between human beings and their life together in society. It was, in short, an ethical analysis. How should one be a good sexual being? By practicing the virtues of continence and prudence. What are the opposite vices? Foolishness and lust.

A dramatic shift in perspective is demanded when we begin to talk about sin, as distinct from vice. Now the horizon is not simply relations among us, but our relationship to God. For Christianity, this is the fundamental and critical meaning of sin. The diseases of freedom which vices reveal derive from a more fundamental corruption, namely the distortion of one's relationship with God.

For Christians, sin in the proper sense is singular rather than plural. It is the hardened idolatrous impulse that refuses God's claim on the world, and on me. Because of that refusal—that original and generative falsehood—all other relationships become poisoned. It is because I willfully reject my condition as a creature utterly dependent on God every moment for my very existence, that my perception of all the rest of the world becomes twisted. For those of us who stand under the judgment of the Living God, sin is not a series of disparate acts so much as it is a fundamental rebellion, a disposition that organizes all our acts into patterns of deceit and infidelity. There are not, then, many sins, but one sin with many and malicious masks.

What sort of deadly disease of the soul do we meet, then, in avarice, our sin of the day? The first thing to note is that it is a remarkably democratic sin, universal in its appeal, manifold in its expression. The word avarice derives from the Latin a*varitia*, which emphasizes its "desirous" dimension. In the New Testament, we meet it in its Greek dress as *pleonexia*, which suggests an insatiable quest for possession. Avarice is the endless wanting of more. Wanting more is both understandable and almost universal among humans. Who of us does not want more, of something?

Among ancient Greek moralists, avarice was regarded as an illness of natural human appetite, a disordered grasping after things, and most of all, money, because then as now, money could buy almost anything else. The imbalance of the spirit called avarice did not simply want things, it wanted them at any cost to others. In some contexts, indeed, the term *pleonexia* could mean simply to seek an advantage over others. If I get more, you get less. This vice was repugnant to Greek ethicists because it offended their instinct for good order and equity. And they recognized in avarice an element of hostility toward others, reflected in a competitiveness that could quickly turn violent.

Aristotle and Plutarch, in fact, would quickly have identified the vice of avarice in those money changers Jesus drove out of the temple in today's Gospel—see? I did sneak a reading in! It was not enough for them to have religious status because of their association with temple sacrifices. They needed as well to fleece tourists and pilgrims to make a monetary profit as well.

But as Christians, and not as ancient moralists, we need to ask how avarice is properly a manifestation of sin, which we have defined in terms of a fundamental refusal of God's claim on our lives. Allow me to suggest that the desire to *have* more at whatever cost to another stems from the need to *be* more. Having is equated with being, owning more is being more, a larger house means a greater person.

Once I have refused to accept my existence and worth as gift from another, this is a necessary equation for me to make. Faced with the terror of contingency—which means that I could just as easily not exist as exist at all, or for that matter, continue to exist—faced with this terrible realization, I am driven to try to construct and secure my own being and worth. And this means gathering everything I can find within my control, so that I will know that I am, and that I am significant. "I must be real; look at how many things I have." Possessing, in short, becomes idolatrous; owning and having become absolutes. Without this *having*, I might fall out of being altogether.

Logically, this equation of being and having connects avarice to the vice (or sin) of envy, in which the hostility embedded in avarice finds overt expression. If you have more than me, you are more than me, you are better than me. This is a world of limited goods, there is only so much to go around. We are competitors for those limited goods. Therefore, I need to bring you down to my level, or even eliminate you as my rival altogether. Avarice and envy have as their ultimate expression violence, social unrest, war, and murder.

As in all idolatry, the finite thing that I treat as absolute demands constant service from me. I need to devote all my energies to propping up an idol that has no life of its own but necessarily sucks life from its worshipers. My possessions must be maintained and protected. The stakes, after all, are ultimate. Avarice, then, does not mean simply the pursuit of money, but the effort to secure my very existence by means of any form of possession, which can include not only bank accounts and houses and fancy cars, but also friends and lovers and family and ideas and time and space and health and even virtue!

Avarice can even drive us to make our relationship with God idolatrous, that is, something we own and can therefore control. In this most sophisticated version of the sin, as Paul tells the Romans just before the passage we read today—see, I did it again!—it can even make the commandments of God into an opportunity for acquisitiveness (Rom 2:17–24). We obey him in order to bribe him when he judges. We demand of God payment for the worth we have earned by our possessions (Rom 11:33–36). Now the vice of avarice is potentiated into sin, and can be seen not only as a rebellion against God, but as the fundamental rebellion underlying all the others: I don't need a gift from you, I am earning my own way by what I acquire!

How, then, is avarice a "deadly" sin? Because avarice is based on an illusion, an empty fantasy, a lie. To serve the idol of possessing is to die. The idol cannot give life; possessions cannot extend our existence. The idol neither has life itself nor can bestow life and worth. It lives at all only by draining its servants of their energy and life.

Only the Living God, the source of all that is or ever has been or ever will be, can create and sustain us, and can raise us to new life. The good news we celebrate together today is that we are, in fact, not on our own, we do not exist on the basis of what we possess. We are, and always have been, gifted by the presence and power of God, by the love of God poured into our hearts by the Holy Spirit. So as Jesus revealed to us the very life of God by his self-emptying availability to the needs of others, by his not grasping his life but flinging it freely in service to his neighbor, the Spirit that comes to us from him enables us to loosen the frozen grip of our fingers around what we think we possess, and gives us life that is true life.

Our being and worth has been established already by gift. It need only be accepted. We need only say "yes." And instead of saying to the darkness, "I want," we can say, "Thank you," to the light. And be free.

REPENTANCE[1]

Luke 13:1–9

My sisters and brothers in Christ, the section of Luke's Gospel from which today's reading comes shows Jesus on a long journey. The prophet who makes his way from Galilee to Jerusalem also moves toward the death that awaits all those who challenge the world with God's vision for the world.

And as Jesus presses toward his destiny, repeatedly telling his followers of the necessity of his death and of his certainty concerning his vindication, he also intensifies his prophetic mission. To the crowds surrounding him, he issues calls to repentance; to the opponents seeking to entrap him, he tells parables that illustrate the consequences of the failure to repent; and to the disciples who follow in his path, he gives instructions concerning the deeds of repentance: sharing possessions, praying in all circumstances, persevering in the face of persecution.

Luke's literary depiction of Jesus journeying to his death on Passover provides the perfect metaphor for the church's practice of Lent, in which believers imagine the forty days from Ash Wednesday to Easter as steps on a journey that they take toward the paschal mystery. But Lenten observance falls short if it is only a form of liturgical imagination, of ritual enactment.

The church has always understood that the deeper correspondence is between Jesus's real journey to God through his suffering and death, and the believer's very real passage through the moments of life as a journey to God that must pass through suffering and death. As Saint Benedict says in his *Rule* for monks, "All of life should have a certain Lenten character." He means that the real business of Lent, and the real business of life, is the business of repentance.

---

1. Preached at Cannon Chapel, Candler School of Theology to faculty, staff, and students, 2015.

REPENTANCE

The term "repentance" (*metanoia*) is often and correctly translated as a "change of mind," for such it is. In Luke's Gospel, this change of mind means receiving as one's own the prophet's word concerning God's vision for the world; it means revising the norms of the world constructed by humans on their own terms, the norms that measure success and happiness in terms of pleasure, power, and possessions and that measure piety in terms of cultivating the self and excluding the other.

To accept God's measure of the world announced by the prophet Jesus is to reckon as happy those who are poor and hungry, who grieve, who are persecuted rather than popular; it means to consider piety in terms of humbling the self and exalting the other.

But for Luke's Gospel, repentance is not authentic if it remains only a change in perspective. It is genuine repentance when that change of mind and heart is embodied by practices corresponding to God's vision for humanity, in a manner of life that shares possessions, travels lightly, prays for discernment, and leads others through self-emptying service.

Repentance becomes effective, moreover, when it is enacted through a ministry of healing that is extended to all those excluded from the world's favor: the sick, the demon-possessed, the dying, and all those shut out through the arrogance of belonging, like the little ones of children and women and strangers, and all those the presumptuousness of piety declares unclean and sinful.

If repentance meant only getting right with God, then it might be done in an instant; but if repentance means getting right with God's world, then it demands what Luke calls the works of repentance.

If repentance meant only a change of mind, then it could be done easily and quickly; but if repentance requires a change of life itself, then it requires all the time we have given to us, and we must start at once.

The gift of mortal life is the gift of time. Time is given us for the sake of repentance, so that we can become rightly aligned with God and God's world. This is the essential and irreplaceable task of our life, and the task we have been given.

Yet time is, of all gifts, the easiest one to let slip through our fingers. We pass time, spend time, waste time, kill time, with all the trivial chores we convince ourselves are essential to accomplish, and thus allow ourselves to be distracted from the one truly essential task of the time we have been given, for to die without repentance is to miss the entire point of having lived at all.

And because time, of all the gifts we have been given, is the one least within our control, can slip away entirely before we are ready, while we are yet distracted, and with great inconvenience, the task of repentance takes on ultimate seriousness and urgency. This was understood by Jewish sages. Rabbi Eliezer is reported as declaring that one should repent the day before dying.[2] But his disciples improved on his statement by observing that one could die any day without warning, so that all of life should be one of repentance.[3]

It is with this same understanding, though with a typically prophetic sharpness, that Jesus addresses the crowd on the way to Jerusalem, and addresses us today with the words we have just read.

The first two sayings in the passage speak directly to our human condition. Jesus speaks from the headlines of his day. They had heard of those killed by Pilate while they were performing their sacrifices, and they have heard of those on whom the tower at Siloam had fallen. They are not to think of such events as punishment for sin. What makes such events tragic is not death, for death comes to all, but that death came so suddenly and without warning, so that there was no chance to repent. Life is not only ended in such cases, it is ended without a point if those dying were not in right relation to god and God's creation. If his hearers don't repent, Jesus says, then they will perish in the same way—meaning, their lives also will have been wasted.

The point of these jarring examples is to make the listeners aware of the tenuousness of their hold on the time they have been given; it can vanish without warning.

If he had spoken from today's headlines, Jesus might have said, "Those people at a Batman movie who were savagely and senselessly slaughtered in Aurora, Colorado, were no better or worse than anyone else; they did not die because they were sinners. Or those people caught without warning by the tsunami in Thailand: they were neither better nor worse than us. They did not die as punishment for sins. But the sudden and shocking character of their deaths should remind us that we also might die tomorrow, and must therefore repent today, might indeed die today, and thus must repent now."

The lesson is not to avoid the movies or the beach. The lesson is that repentance is the single task for which we have each been assigned a limited

2. Pirke Aboth 2.10.
3. b. TShab 153a.

and unknowable length of time, and must therefore must come before anything else.

At the close of today's reading, Luke appropriates the figure of the barren fig tree, which in the Gospels of Matthew and Mark (Matt 21:18–19; Mark 11:12–14, 20) is connected to a prophetic act of Jesus and turned to a logion on judgment. Luke reports it as a parable that Jesus uses as commentary on his warnings to repent.

The parable takes the perspective, not of those whose time is short, but of the One who gives them time—that is, existence itself—for the sole purpose that they bear fruit.

The language of fruit-bearing, in fact, echoes John the Baptist's demand for repentance even before Jesus started his ministry. John declared, "The axe is laid to the root of the tree, so that any tree which fails to bear good fruit will be cut down and thrown on the fire" (Luke 3:9). When John is then asked by people what they should do, he responds with the same demands concerning possessions that we later find in the mouth of Jesus (Luke 3:10–14). The fruits that God expects are the fruits of repentance, the dispositions and actions that correspond to the prophetic announcement of God's vision for humanity.

At first glance, Jesus's parable resembles other ancient statements concerning God's providence by philosophers like Plutarch.[4] In answer to the question why God does not punish sinners but allows them to live, the defenders of God's providence respond that was appears to be God's delay in justice is actually a manifestation of God's patience and mercy: God allows sinners more time in the hope that they will repent and become righteous rather than unrighteous. In the New Testament we find the point made by 2 Pet 3:9 and Rom 2:4.

The difference in Jesus's parable is that here it is the owner of the tree who is impatient and wants it cut down immediately because of its failure to bear fruit. It is the gardener, the one who tends the trees, who begs for an extension of time, and pledges himself to dig round it and feed it with manure, in the hope that it will yet bear some fruit. But even the gardener recognizes that the delay can only be temporary: "Next year, if it does not bear fruit, then cut it down."

Does the figure of the gardener suggest to you—as it does to me—the prophet Jesus himself, who even as he moves toward his own death, exhorts those he meets on the road, seeking by every means available to make them

---

4. Plutarch, *On the Divine Vengeance*.

see what is God's vision for them, and how God seeks for them to live according to that vision, before the chance to repent is no longer available? By placing the parable within the narrative context he himself has constructed, the evangelist appears to invite such a connection.

Of far greater importance than that literary conceit, however, of far greater moment than the coherence of this sermon, of far more weight than whether we keep our Lenten resolutions, of far more significance than anything you and I do today—whether it is writing papers or grading papers, deciding to come to Candler or deciding for another school, whether we succeed at our many tasks or fail at them—is that we repent and do the works of repentance. For the gift of time has been given us for this one purpose, and failing to do this, we fail utterly.

HOLY WEEK

THE CROSS AND CHRISTIAN EXISTENCE[1]

Hebrews 9:11–15

My sisters and brothers in Christ, Christians have traditionally conceived of Holy Week as a time of intense preparation for Easter. They have understood that the good news of Christ's resurrection—his exaltation to the presence and power of God and his continued presence and power among us through the Holy Spirit—involves also the far more paradoxical good news of his passion and death.

They have grasped, though not always gladly, that their own participation in the paschal mystery—not only liturgically in this Lenten season, but also existentially in every season of their lives—also necessarily means passing through their own suffering and death as prelude to fully sharing in the glory that is the presence and power of God.

Christians have also traditionally read, and even performed, the four passion narratives of the Gospels during the days of Holy Week, as a reminder not only of what God had done for them in Jesus Christ, but also as a dramatic but nonetheless true way of participating, moment by moment, in his path of suffering.

This Holy Week at All Saints, we are entering the mystery through a slightly different form of scriptural imagination. We are not reading the Gospels, which speak of Jesus's cross as a story in the past, but are rather reading parts of early Christian letters, two from Paul's First Letter to the Corinthians, and two from the anonymous Letter to the Hebrews (sent in the same period and possibly even to the same people). These scraps of letters speak of the cross of Jesus in terms of its present significance for their lives as believers in the resurrection.

---

1. This is the first of four sermons delivered on the first four days after Palm Sunday, to All Saints Episcopal Church in downtown Atlanta, Georgia, in 2012.

Those first believers were probably much more convinced than we are of the power of the resurrection. They were, after all, only recently drawn into the energy field of the Holy Spirit that was the church. But no less than us, they needed reminding of the other part of the good news, concerning the passion and death of Jesus. How could this splendid gift come to them through the ugliness and shame of a state execution that combined torture and asphyxiation?

This section of Hebrews (9:11–15) that we read this morning is especially difficult for us, possibly much more difficult for us than for its first audience. Jesus's death is here expressed through imagery that is totally foreign to us, and within an imaginative vision of the world no longer ours.

The imagery is that of ancient temple sacrifice, specifically the slaughter of animals whose blood was offered to God. Sacrifice is not a common term in our contemporary lexicon. We consider it less as a path to God than as a way of misshaping humans.

Hebrews places this—to us offensive—imagery of sacrifice within an imaginative universe drawn from both the philosopher Plato and the Jewish Scripture. Plato imagined the world of ideas, what we might call the spiritual world, as more real, more true, and infinitely better than the world of matter we inhabit. Jews influenced by Plato—and the author of Hebrews was certainly one of them—could imagine the biblical "heaven," where God dwells, in terms of such spiritual, immaterial perfection, and the "earth," where we dwell, in terms of mere materiality, passing away, imperfect, only a pale shadow of what is truly real.

All of this is alien enough. But then Hebrews goes a step further. The author takes the architecture of the ancient temple in Jerusalem—the place where sacrifices were made—and turns it from horizontal to vertical. The here and now of our mortal lives is imagined as the outer court of the temple. The true sanctuary is in heaven, that is, where God dwells.

And having accomplished this complex and daring act of imagination, Hebrews then portrays the death of Jesus, that terrible gasping suffocation on that horrible lonely hill, as the perfect sacrifice offered by his body—not the blood of animals but his own blood—that enters with his ascent to the Father into the perfect heavenly sanctuary, where the effect of his obedient self-donation for us remains efficacious forever.

Candor forces us to admit that all of this seems not only strange to us, it seems even slightly bizarre. Our universe is not one imagined by Plato, but one described by Francis Bacon. Technology and commerce, not philosophy, steer our calculations and action. What counts for us is not what is unseen but what is seen, what can be grasped, measured, counted, assigned a price. Reality for us is not in heaven, it is here on earth. Not the sacrifice of the self, moreover, but the acquisition of a lifestyle is what we regard as realistic. Not eternal perfection but a temporary advantage is what we are taught by the mechanisms of political competition and day-trading. We do not so much pursue the cleansing of our conscience as the covering of our tracks.

Here, then, is the first gift this ancient text gives us. It challenges us to consider whether its universe or ours is the larger and more adequate. Is the world we have fashioned and which fashions us, the world of slippery conviction and temporary commitment, the world of never-ending novelty and inevitable boredom, the world of get-what-you-can and repent on Oprah only when you get caught, is this world actually more real, more true, better, than the world imagined by Hebrews?

Our world enables us to do wonderful things while we are young and healthy and have material resources, but it cannot deal with age and sickness and poverty and loss. Above all, it cannot enable us to imagine death—the mystery we all face—as anything except ultimate closure.

But Hebrews has taken the most offensive of all deaths, that of the only fully innocent human, and imagined it as an opening to what is most real, most true, most beautiful, and all good—an opening to the presence and power of God. There is nothing in the day-trader's manual or in the congressional record that encourages such an imaginative leap.

This text of Scripture, though, offers us a way of thinking, a way of imagining, a larger world than that of give-and-take. It pictures the world as one in which the unseen God is the premise and goal of all that we do in this all-too-solid realm of give-and-take, and that makes all the difference. It enables us to treat the realm of give-and-take not as ultimate and all-consuming—forget about adequate or true—but as relative and temporary, and measured by the unseen presence and power that calls it at every moment into being.

Hebrews does more than offer us the chance to consider an alternative way of imaging the world. It points us to the most profound significance of Christ's death, as it pertains to each one of us.

The Platonic contrast between spiritual and material is not, for Hebrews, simply, or even essentially a contrast between "down here" and "up there." The Unseen God is not in a place, but suffuses every place, does not occupy a space among other spaces but is the power that sustains all spaces. The contrast that Hebrews helps us think about is the one between the exterior and the interior of our human lives, although even here, the spatial terms "interior" and "exterior" can distort what he is getting at. Yet Hebrews and we need some such terms to get at the reality he seeks to express.

Let's start with the exterior. The sacrifices of the ancient Jewish cult involved the blood and meat of animals. They are outside humans, although humans put them forward to represent themselves to God. And what the ancient cult accomplished, says Hebrews, was also external. It defined the boundaries of the people. The cult signified who was in and who was out societally. Participation in the cult was necessary to belong to the people of Israel. Such is a perfectly legitimate religious activity and goal. But it is external. It makes the people "holy," that is, distinct from other populations. But it was never designed to change people's hearts. Nor did it do so.

Hebrews argues that because God in Christ entered fully into our human existence, got inside us, so to speak, Jesus's faithful response to God, the obedience that made him a perfect Son, changes our human existence as well. His sacrifice is in his own blood and requires his own personal choice. Hebrews says that when Christ came into the world it was with the cry, "I have come to do your will, O God," and notes that it is by this will that we are saved. Jesus's sacrifice, in a word, demanded of him an interior and not simply exterior commitment, a response from his heart.

The effect, Hebrews says, is that our own hearts now have the capacity to respond to God in the same way. Our consciences, that is, our deepest senses of individual freedom and responsibility, have been cleansed, so that we are capable of responding to the unseen God in precisely the way that Jesus did. His sacrifice does not mark the external boundaries of a people. It purifies and empowers the internal dispositions of individual believers.

For Hebrews, the death of Jesus is one in which he is at once victim and priest. It is a new opening "in the flesh" between God and humans. It establishes the covenant about which Jeremiah the prophet had dreamed: "I will place my laws in their minds and I will write them on their hearts; I will be their God and they will be my people. And they shall not teach their fellow citizens or their brothers, saying, 'Know the Lord,' for all shall know me from least to greatest. I will forgive their evildoing, and their sins I will remember no more" (Jer 31:31–34; Heb 8:10–12). Such, says Hebrews, is the effect of Jesus's death that he died "once for all" in our behalf.

The world Hebrews imagines is difficult for us today to imagine. The gift of Christ that Hebrews describes is difficult for us to accept, for to accept it means that we must focus our attention, not on the external appearances of our lives, but on the internal integrity of our thoughts, our dispositions, and our commitments.

We must pay attention not to how good we look to others, or even at times to ourselves, but to how we appear to the One of whom Hebrews speaks, who is "living and effective, sharper than any two-edged sword, [who] penetrates and divides soul and spirit, joints and marrow, [who] judges the reflections and thoughts of the heart. Nothing is concealed from him; all lies bare and exposed to the eyes of him to whom we must render an account" (4:12–13). It is small wonder that Hebrews also declares, "It is a fearful thing to fall into the hands of the living God" (10:31).

THE POWER OF THE CROSS[1]

1 Corinthians 1:18–31

My brothers and sisters in Christ, during this Holy Week at All Saints we are meditating on the passion and death of Jesus, not in the traditional manner through the recitation of the passion narratives, but by hearing and thinking about passages from letters written by leaders to first-generation believers who struggled to hold together the two parts of the good news.

They were all too happy to accept that God was giving them new power through the Holy Spirit that came to them because of the resurrection of Jesus and his exaltation as Lord. But they struggled, perhaps even more than we do, with the part of the saving message concerning the crucifixion of Jesus. I say "perhaps," because after considering this morning Paul's words to the Corinthians, we might ask ourselves if we are really that much different than the readers he addresses some twenty-five years after Jesus was executed.

They should have struggled more than we do because they lived in a world in which the state authority used crucifixion not only to kill but also to shame its enemies. Whereas it is conceivable for us to wear a cross on a chain as a piece of jewelry, an adornment that brings admiration to the one wearing it, they could only perceive the cross for what it still was, a Roman instrument of torture for the outcast of society—slaves and revolutionaries—specifically designed to bring humiliation to the ones so executed and to anyone associated with them.

Joining a commune based on a crucified messiah in the first century was not unlike our joining a cult based on a contemporary state-executed criminal like Gary Gilmore. Anyone seeking to join the cult for its social

---

1. Preached on the Tuesday of Holy Week 2012 at All Saints Episcopal in Atlanta; second in a series of four.

benefits would rightly pause to consider the downside: do we want to share the stigma of the state execution of our founder?

In his first letter to the church at Corinth—about eight hundred miles from Jerusalem, where Jesus was executed—Paul addresses believers who relish the power coming to them from the resurrection, but can't grasp the implications of the fact that this power came from the cross.

Joining the assembly from a world in which social status was carefully calibrated in terms of lineage, education, wealth, power, and reputation—how things have changed!—the Corinthians assumed that life within this new association would also recognize and protect the same indicators of social standing. What point is there to joining a club that does not recognize or even elevate our status?

Paul perceives, in fact, that his readers have made the ritual of baptism—the sacrament of immersion into the death as well as the resurrection of Christ—into a marker in their competitive game: who was initiated by a more important cult leader than another? "I am Paul's," "Hah! I belong to Apollos," "Well, I am Peter's," "Of yeah? Well, I'm Christ's!" (1:12).

Before he can start them thinking with what he calls "the mind of Christ" (2:26), then, Paul must get them to seriously engage the part of the good news they are suppressing, what he calls "the word of the cross" (1:18).

Paul starts with the bold assertion that the word of the cross is foolishness to those who are perishing, but "to those of us who are being saved," it is "the power of God." What outsiders perceive one way, insiders perceive another.

It is striking that Paul does not then move at once to the insider perspective but to the outsider point of view. Perhaps he suggests that these new converts so enamored of their social position even within the church continue to think more like outsiders than true insiders.

What is the outsider perspective on Jesus's death on the cross? Paul distinguishes between gentile outsiders and Jewish outsiders. To gentiles, the cross is foolishness. To Jews, it is a stumbling block. Why? Because, Paul says, gentiles seek wisdom and Jews seek signs. Paul speaks so cryptically here that we must do some decoding to understand.

First, the gentiles: ancient polytheists would not at all cringe at the proclamation of Jesus as God's Son because of the resurrection. They honored a fair number of humans who had likewise joined the extended family of the gods. But there were requirements needing to be met. Only sages who displayed great wisdom (like a Socrates) or leaders who displayed divine powers (like emperors) deserved such posthumous glory.

Measured by such criteria, Jesus's manner of death disqualified him from divine honors. He was fearful, he did not eloquently defend himself, he was abandoned by his followers, and his death was the shameful one imposed on slaves. How could divine power and wisdom be associated with such obvious folly?

The Jews, Paul says, seek signs. We misunderstand if we suppose that he is here thinking of spectacular miracles. He means that Jews seek signs that Jesus is the Messiah. The basic criterion would be that he made things better for the Jews. He didn't. From their perspective, therefore, Jesus is at best a failed messiah. But worse, the manner of his life suggests that he was not even a good Torah-observant Jew: he worked on the Sabbath and associated with sinners and tax collectors. And his crucifixion proved that he could not be the source of life and power that Christians claimed. Torah itself proclaimed as cursed anyone who was hanged upon a tree (Deut 21:23). Those who proclaimed him the Holy One blasphemed. This is indeed a stumbling block.

Paul elaborates on the scandal of the cross to outsiders precisely because those to whom he is speaking—those now being saved by the good news—are themselves gentiles and Jews. They have carried with them into this new association all their prior perceptions of how God should work: with majesty, with manifest power, with great wisdom, and primarily among the well-established in the world. Even among new believers, the cross is foolishness and a stumbling block, for it offends their sense of what is fitting to the divine.

How natural it was for them, and indeed for us, to gloss over this offensive part of the message from God and focus only on the energy, the power, the elevation of our own lives through the Spirit. How natural for them, indeed for us, having once passed through the foolishness and scandal of the cross, to adopt our customary markers and measure of worth, even within the church, so that the church acts, as it decently should, according to "the wisdom of the world."

But, Paul thunders, the wisdom of the world did not get us to the living God! It got us only to the wretched projections of ourselves that in turn distorted us and the world. Since we could not get to God through our own notions of reality and what is fitting to the divine ("the wisdom of the world"), Paul declares, God had to get to us, had to reach out and touch us in a manner that would show us, once for all, that God's ways are not our ways.

So, God touched us in the manner of life led by Jesus and the specific mode of death Jesus suffered. In the cross, Jesus revealed "the wisdom of God." And predictably, Paul states, the rulers of this world did not recognize the one they crucified. The wisdom of God and the wisdom of the world collide at the cross.

Paul's exhortation to his readers is just as provocative, just as counterintuitive an appeal to the imagination, as that issued by Hebrews in the passage we read yesterday. No less than Hebrews does Paul appeal to an understanding of the world that directly conflicts with the one we ordinarily assume to be true. Of course, we say, the world is run on the basis of pleasure and possessions and prestige and power. And if the church is part of the world, then the same standards naturally apply here as well.

But both Paul and Hebrews tell us that our understanding of reality is deficient because it leaves out of account the way in which God has actually displayed both power and wisdom, through the weakness and foolishness of a single human being's suffering and shameful execution. The pattern of the cross is the pattern of God's activity in the world; it is not the exception, it is God's rule.

If such is the source of the power that now calls them into a new existence and enables them to live in an entirely new manner, then, Paul argues, God's foolishness is wiser than any human wisdom we can conjure, and God's weakness is stronger than any human force we can manipulate.

As his most convincing proof, Paul appeals to the conditions of their own calling by God into the assembly of believers. They were not, in fact, among the world's elite and sophisticated and powerful; they were—we are, let's face it—not an auspicious lot. Just as God chose to reveal his wisdom and power through a state-executed messiah, so God continues to reveal his paradoxical wisdom and power through a community that arises not from the center of society but from the margins, not from the mighty but from the weak, not from the smart but from the slow. God does this, Paul says, simply to show that the living God summons into existence that which is nothing, or, to put it another way, to show that God is God and we are not.

We are, this spring morning, in a small building surrounded by the massive towers of commercial and political power. We are in a silent space within the noise of a great city. We are not the movers and shakers of this metropolis. Mainly we are the moved and shaken. We are not the smartest people in this city, but among its less clever citizens.

But we claim as our salvation a wisdom and power not our own. We claim, with Paul, that in such small and quiet and lowly spots as this all around the globe this Tuesday of Holy Week, the mighty power and wisdom of God are silently at work to transform creation.

JESUS'S FAITH AND OURS[1]

Hebrews 12:1–9

My sisters and brothers in Christ, we have been observing the first part of Holy Week this year by reading New Testament letters, alternating between Hebrews and First Corinthians. On Monday, Hebrews invited us to imagine a world quite different from our own, and to think of Christ's death as a sacrifice that cleansed our consciences, enabling our hearts to "know God" within a new covenant. On Tuesday, Paul asked us to grasp how the foolishness and weakness of the cross—a stumbling block to all worldly wisdom and an embarrassment to all who live by the wisdom of the world—is the lens through which we must perceive God's way of working in the world. Both ancient writers agree that the cross of Jesus is more than a fact of the past; it is the pattern that shapes our present.

This morning, we hear again from Hebrews. The passage we read is the climax of a section that begins with the statement, "Faith is confident assurance concerning what we hope for, and conviction about things we do not see" (Heb 11:1), and elaborates by adding that faith believes that "the worlds were created by God and what is visible came into being through what is invisible" (11:3).

Hearing these words, we are reminded how this composition imagines the world in terms of an invisible heaven (God's realm) that is more real and more perfect than the visible earth (the realm of the merely mortal), and human existence as directed to that fuller and richer existence which is God's.

The section of Hebrews beginning in 11:1 is addressed to believers who in fact were losing confident assurance concerning their hope, who were indeed less than convinced about things they could not see. Reading

1. Preached on Wednesday of Holy Week, 2012 at All Saints Church, Atlanta; the third in a series of four.

between the lines, we can detect that some of these early Christians were turning away from their first enthusiasm, and even abandoning their assemblies.

Why? The cause of their disaffection seems to have been the weight of harsh experience. They had not been killed for their faith, but they were being mocked because of it. Some of them had been imprisoned. Others had their property confiscated. On top of all these things that brought shame on people in antiquity—just as homelessness and jail bring shame on people today—they drew contempt from outsiders and internalized that contempt. Why contempt? Because they followed a cult leader who had suffered the most shameful of all deaths in antiquity, a death only slaves and losers had to suffer, and if Jesus was a loser, they were losers too, by association. Persecution is much less hard on faith than is mockery. Persecution and martyrdom attack our flesh and bones. Mockery seeps into our minds and makes us ashamed.

The author of Hebrews responds to his hearers sense of shame and their temptation to give up on their faith, by forging another magnificent image of mortal human life as directed toward the living God, an image that has fundamentally shaped all subsequent Christian mysticism and spirituality. He pictures his readers as people on a grand pilgrimage toward God.

They are not on an external, physical journey through material space. Their pilgrimage is one of moral transformation through the moments of their life, as their hearts turn progressively toward their source and destiny, and as their movement toward the invisible God is propelled by faith.

Earlier in the letter, the author had warned his hearers with a negative example of a failed pilgrimage (3:7—4:10). He reminds them of the generation that wandered through the desert after the exodus, and of how many of that generation failed to reach their goal in the promised land precisely because of their lack of faith. But believers in Christ are not making their way to a material territory where they could rest; they are on pilgrimage to God's presence and the Sabbath rest that is God's own life (4:1).

Each step toward that goal is marked by their response of faith in the living God every embodied moment of every mortal day, as the author says, quoting the psalm, "Today if you hear his voice do not harden your hearts as in the wilderness" (3:7).

And immediately before today's lection, which, as we have heard, calls Jesus "the pioneer and perfecter of faith," the author summons as witnesses to such faith—and therefore as positive examples to his readers—all those who did hear the call of God in their lives, and did respond with obedient faith, from Abel to the Maccabees. All of them, our author says, lived "by faith," and all of them received approval from God.

As he is for other New Testament writers, so also for Hebrews, Abraham is the prime example of faith in God. He left his home—became homeless—to wander in a land he did not know, because of his faith in the God who called him. He and his children, Hebrews says, lived in tents, because the homeland they sought was not really the physical country of Canaan—they were already there. Instead, the author declares, Abraham "sojourned in the promised land as in a foreign country, dwelling in tents with Isaac and Jacob, heirs of the same promise, because he was looking forward to a city with foundations, whose designer and maker is God" (11:8–10).

What Abraham truly sought as he wandered the land was his heavenly homeland in the presence of God, what the author calls "a better, heavenly country," and adds, "wherefore God is not ashamed to be called their God, for he has prepared a city for them" (11:16). Our ancestors in the faith were willing to do without home, possessions, and honor because of their faith. Abraham was ready even to sacrifice his only son, Isaac, because he was convinced that God could raise him from the dead (11:17–19).

The struggle for survival among ancient nomads in search of a homeland is for Hebrews the external expression of the process of moral transformation in human hearts through faith. The supreme model for this pilgrimage is Jesus himself, whom the author of Hebrews here calls "pioneer and perfecter of faith." He is pioneer because he goes before us, showing us the way. He is perfecter because he has already arrived where we hope to go.

We remember that Hebrews describes Jesus's exultant cry as he enters the world, "I have come to do your will O Lord" (10:5). But that will turned out to be not easily done. Hebrews speaks of Jesus in the days of his flesh crying out with loud cries and tears. The scene reminds us of the Gospels describing Jesus in his agony before his arrest. The author declares that, although Jesus was God's Son, he learned obedience from the things he suffered, and thus becoming perfect (or mature), he became the source of salvation to those who in turn obey him (5:7–10).

Jesus expresses his obedient faith at the moment of his death, to be sure, but that moment was prepared for by all that he experienced in his life, as he learned in the way we all must, what faith in God truly entails.

Jesus needed to be educated as a son of God, and his lessons involved the pain that is inevitable to growing into full maturity.

In the image of human life as a pilgrimage, Jesus moves before us, as he was transformed moment by moment through his responses to God in every circumstance. And we follow after our pioneer, being transformed moment by moment until death opens us to the presence of God.

Surrounded by the great cloud of witnesses who were the heroes of Israel's faith, then, Jesus showed himself our perfect model; he despised the shame of the cross because of the joy that was placed before him, and enduring the cross, has taken his seat on the right hand of the throne of God. Let us, says Hebrews, keep our eyes on Jesus.

Right after the passage we read this morning, then, Hebrews turns to exhort his readers—and us—who out of weariness at the length of the journey or shame at our commitments, are tempted to abandon the assembly and quit the pilgrimage altogether. He continues the image of the race that was suggested by the phrase "great cloud of witnesses"—think of the stadium filled with people at the end of a Olympic marathon. We are to "run the race that is set before us" as we look ahead at Jesus, the pioneer. Hebrews tell us to lift our drooping hands and strengthen our weak knees so that what is lame may not be out of joint but healed (12:12–13).

But why should we summon our energy and move forward on a journey that seems much harder than an Olympic marathon, seems to involve so much pain and shame that we sometimes cannot even imagine the joy that lies before us?

Hebrews answers this question by reminding his readers—and us—that what we suffer in our mortal lives is a kind of education that God reserves for his legitimate children. Just as Jesus, although God's Son learned obedience through what he suffered, and thus reached maturity, so are we to recognize in our hard instruction the sort of discipline that the Lord uses to educate the children he loves and lead them to maturity.

You are enduring for the sake of an education, Hebrews reminds us (11:5). God is treating us as sons, and if we endure to the end, then, with Jesus, who despised the shame of the cross and kept his eye on the joy set before him, we too will enter fully into the presence of the invisible God, who summons us through what can be seen, at every moment, indeed today.

THE TABLE OF THE LORD[1]

1 Corinthians 11:23–26

My brothers and sisters in Christ, as a way of focusing our attention on the first part of the paschal mystery—the suffering and death of Jesus our Lord—we have spent this first part of Holy Week thinking with passages from first-century letters that were written to communities of believers which were glad to have been empowered by the Holy Spirit, but less than eager to embrace the truth that the work of the Spirit among them was to shape their lives in a manner that made the cross of Christ more than a fact of the past, but the very pattern of their present existence.

The scandal of the cross, we have learned, is not the exception to God's way in the world, it is the rule. And as we have heard Paul and the author of Hebrews address the circumstances and struggles of their long-ago readers, we have come to realize that, in these fundamental matters, we are not so very different from them, and that the word of God spoken by these letters speaks as directly to us as it did to them.

This morning we hear how Jesus himself interpreted his death in the words he spoke to his students at a quiet last meal only hours or even minutes before his arrest, trial, and execution. We hear Jesus speaking, however, not as we usually do within the Gospel narrative, but as quoted by Paul in his first letter to the believers in Corinth.

This is the earliest evidence we possess for the actual words of Jesus, cited by Paul some twenty years after Jesus's death, and some twenty years before the Gospels are written. Paul quotes these words as having come to him "from the Lord," and his version is remarkably close to the versions found in the Synoptic Gospels, above all Luke's.

---

1. Preached at All Saints Episcopal Church on Thursday of Holy Week, 2012; last in a series of four.

Jesus's words to his followers at the meal tell us not only that he willingly accepts the destiny that God has assigned him—in the Gospel, the giving of the cup at the meal is followed by Jesus's acceptance of the cup in the garden—but that he understands his violent death as a sacrifice offered to God for others. In this passage and in the Gospels, Jesus himself provides the deepest inner meaning of the cross. Taking the bread as symbol of his body (his self, his very life), he first blesses it, that is, gives thanks to God (for the bread, for his body, for his life), and then breaks it. And as he breaks it, he says, "This is my body which is for you." His body broken in death is the final expression of his life spent in service to and for them.

Jesus's death does not betray his character but reveals it. Every moment of faithful obedience to God in the small moments of his life, every act of compassion toward others with his own needs left unmet, is brought to perfect expression in his death; the joints and ligaments he bent in care of the weak are now stretched to the breaking; the breaths with which he breathed words of comfort and healing are now ended with a final prayer.

Jesus's words make even clearer his understanding of himself as God's instrument. The cup of his suffering that he will accept and then drink fully is the blood of a new covenant. We catch in his words what the author of Hebrews captured in our first reading when he pictured Jesus's death as a sacrifice not in the blood of animals but in his own blood, and in which not the covenant with Moses is confirmed but the new covenant dreamed by Jeremiah is realized. A covenant in which all humans have their hearts purified and can know God, are not merely defined as a people but are transformed from within.

The fact that Paul should remember and quote these words of Jesus is remarkable enough, evidence all by itself of how important the human Jesus was for the apostle. He refers the sayings of Jesus so seldom. And this is the only time Paul quotes Jesus word for word. Clearly, these words in particular represented for Paul the inner meaning of the cross provided by Jesus himself. But it is the context in which he applies these words that shows how for Paul the cross of Jesus, interpreted as the self-donation of Jesus to others, should be the pattern that guides behavior within the community.

Earlier in the letter, in his discussion of eating foods offered to idols, Paul says that a member of the community who exercises his or her freedom in a manner to cause another member to be shaken in their consciences is hurting "the brother for whom Christ died," and concludes, "when you thus sin against your brothers and wound their weak consciences, you are sinning against Christ."

In order to appreciate the force of Paul's quotation of Jesus, we need to remember the extraordinarily powerful understanding he has of the meal he calls the Lord's supper. For Paul, any gathering of the community provides an opportunity for the spirit of the resurrected Jesus to be present. The church is most explicitly the body of Christ when it gathers communally, for the spirit needs a body in order to express itself. Thus, when those who had drunk the same spirit gathered as Christ's body, the gifts of the Holy Spirit could express themselves through prophecy, teaching, singing, and speaking in tongues.

When the body of Christ gathers to share its ritual meal, the intensity of the bond between the risen Christ and believers is even greater. Earlier in his letter, Paul warned his readers about participating in pagan worship because of the spiritual entanglements it involves—a kind of fellowship with demons. He bases that argument on his highly realistic sense of what happens in the Christian meal. He asks them, "The cup of blessing that we bless, is it not a fellowship in the blood of Christ? And is not the bread we break a fellowship in the body of Christ?" The fellowship between believers and the risen Lord is real. Christ is present at the meal. What they eat and drink is a participation in his presence through the spirit.

But the fellowship is also with each other: "Because the loaf of bread is one, we, many though we are, are one body, for we all partake one loaf." We see the dense and interconnected levels. The bread that symbolizes the body of the crucified one, the body of the community that expresses the spirit of the risen one, the bread broken and shared that expresses the unity of this body to Christ and to each other. The entire meaning of this meal for Paul is fellowship, that is, sharing and unity.

It is against this understanding of the Eucharist that we can appreciate Paul's rebuke of the Corinthians concerning their conduct at the Lord's supper. "I cannot praise you," he says, "because your gatherings are not profitable but harmful." They are harmful because the Corinthians have once more carried the attitudes and behaviors characteristic of the larger world into the assembly. First, they display at this meal the same divisiveness that Paul rebuked at the start of the letter. When he speaks of different factions among them, we can picture the parish fellowship meals at which folks only eat with their friends, or worse, only talk with those who have voted with them in the latest church crisis. So they destroy the ideal of unity that the bread and cup signify.

Second, they carry into the Lord's supper the discriminatory practices built into the ancient system of patronage. Those who were wealthy and powerful—who may well have provided the food for the common meal—were according to the ancient protocol, those who ate first and best, while those who received their benefits ate last and least. And even this practice seems to be abused, with some of the wealthy getting drunk, while those with no resources go hungry. If the issue was just eating one's own meal in private, Paul says, they could do that in their own households. The whole point of the meal is the expression of fellowship, of equality, each to each and each before the Lord. Paul declares such behavior "shows contempt for the church of God and shames those who have nothing." He says, "I cannot praise you in this matter."

It is precisely at this point that Paul quotes the words of Jesus, and he concludes his citation with this statement, "Every time then, you eat this bread and drink this cup, you proclaim the death of the Lord until he comes. This means that whoever eats the bread or drinks the cup of the Lord unworthily sins against the body and blood of the Lord . . . he who eats and drinks without recognizing the body eats and drinks a judgment on himself."

The pattern of the cross, says Paul, must also be the pattern of community behavior. When Jesus blessed and broke the bread it signified the body he gave for others. It falsifies the meaning of the meal to fail to share possessions or to seek one's own position over that of others. Only if those at the meal give their bodies to each other in the manner of Christ do they "recognize the body," that is the church. Those who act in a manner that brings harm or shame to the weak of the church "sin against Christ."

PUTTING THE BODY
WHERE THE MOUTH IS[1]

Luke 19:45–48

"Put your money where your mouth is," we say, when we want someone to show how serious they are about something. It might be a baseball game or a political contest. "Put up or shut up," we say. We think speech unserious that doesn't have some risk attached to it. Could be our money, could be our home, could be our reputation, could be our life itself.

We call certain people prophets because they put their bodies and not just their speech on the line. Mahatma Gandhi peacefully resisted the power of the mighty British empire with marches and strikes. He was assassinated for his efforts. Martin Luther King learned peaceful resistance from Christ and from Gandhi. He was attacked and imprisoned and then assassinated. The Berrigan brothers peacefully protested the Vietnam war, and Philip spent years in prison. Dorothy Day ladled out her life in soup spoons to the derelicts of the Bowery in the name of Christ, dying as poor as those she served.

Real prophets do more than write opinion pieces in the *New Yorker*, or speak to captive audiences. They embody what they profess even at peril to themselves.

On Palm Sunday, the church liturgically re-enacts Jesus's entry as king into Jerusalem. This event, as we all know, inaugurates the final period of conflict between Jesus and the religious authorities that leads to his crucifixion on Friday. Crucifixion was a distinctively Roman mode of execution that the empire reserved for slaves, and those they wanted to mark, and mock, as slaves, like Jews who were prophetic troublemakers.

---

1. Preached on Monday of Holy Week, 2019, All Saints Church, Atlanta; the first of two.

The Gospel of Luke, which we read Sunday and today, certainly wants us to see Jesus's entry into Jerusalem as a royal procession. Alone among the evangelists, Luke places immediately before this entry Jesus's parable of the pounds (19:11–27), which is better understood as a parable about a king triumphing over his opponents. It is told in response to his disciples' query as to whether the kingdom of God was to appear immediately. Luke's Gospel alone has Jesus explicitly called "king" by the crowd of disciples greeting him as he approaches the city (19:38). Luke alone has Jesus at the last supper compare himself to earthly kings, and then bestow royal authority on his disciples (22:24–30). In Luke's Gospel alone, when Jesus is crucified under the ironic banner "King of the Jews," does the penitent rebel declare to him, "Remember me when you enter your kingdom," and hear Jesus respond, "Today, you will be with me in paradise" (23:23–40). Without doubt, Luke wants us to perceive Jesus as king. But what kind of king?

To learn the character of Jesus's kingship, we must go back to the very beginning of Jesus's ministry in Luke's Gospel. You will remember that right after he was baptized—when the Holy Spirit descended on him in bodily form—Jesus is led by the Spirit to the wilderness, where he was tested by Satan. Satan offers Jesus rule over all the kingdoms of the earth. All Jesus need do is worship Satan—the one, we understand, who has all these despotisms at his disposal. Quoting the book of Deuteronomy, Jesus responds, "You shall worship the Lord your God; Him alone shall you serve" (Luke 4:5–8).

Jesus will not be a king, Luke tells us, who will exercise visible rule over human empires. He utterly rejects that sort of dominance. He will serve only the Lord who rules all creation as a servant of those whom God makes and moves in mysterious ways.

Filled with the Holy Spirit, Jesus makes his way to his hometown synagogue. There he announces that God has anointed him as Messiah (= the anointed one) through the outpouring of the Holy Spirit upon him, and that he has been sent to proclaim good news to the poor, and liberation to captives (4:16–18). He is, in short, a prophetic messiah, a prophet-king, whose rule is to be in service of the world's most needy.

When he then goes about Galilee "proclaiming the good news of the kingdom of God" (4:43), his first public statement concerning this kingdom takes this form: "Blessed are you poor, for the kingdom of God is yours" (6:20). He also declares blessed those who are hungry and weep, and those who are hated, excluded, insulted, and denounced as evil, for, Jesus says, "their ancestors treated the prophets in the same way" (6:22).

The kingdom of God that Jesus proclaims is, therefore, even in its words, deeply paradoxical. It is not to consist in domination or exploitation of lands and peoples. It is not to increase the privilege enjoyed by the powerful and the wealthy. Instead, it embraces the poor and the grieving and the dispossessed, and because of that embrace, invites exclusion and mockery.

The proclamation also has a sharp negative edge. Jesus also declares a lamentation corresponding to the blessing: "Woe to you who are rich, for you have your consolation now," and this, "woe to you when all speak well of you, for their ancestors treated the false prophets this way" (6:24–26). As his mother, Mary, had sung before his birth, God's mercy to the lowly involves casting down the mighty from their thrones and sending the rich away empty (1:52–53).

Jesus's first proclamation of the kingdom does not end with these blessing and woes. He continues, with words his followers need to ponder often, for, if they were taken seriously and acted out, all the ways in which power is expressed and exercised within human societies would be overturned. His words summarize the prophet's way of measuring within God's rule:

> To you who hear, I say, love your enemies. Do good to those who hate you. Bless those who curse you. Pray for those who mistreat you. To the person who strikes you on one cheek, turn the other one as well. And from the person who takes your cloak, do not withhold even your tunic. Give to everyone who asks from you, and from the one who takes what is yours, do not demand it back. Do to others as you would have them do to you. If you love those who love you, what credit is that to you? Even sinners love those that love them. And if you do good to those who do good to you, what credit is that to you? Even sinners do the same. If you lend money to those from whom you expect repayment, what credit is that to you? Even sinners give to sinners and get back the same amount.
>
> But, rather, love your enemies, and do good to them, and lend expecting nothing back; then your reward will be great, and you will be children of the most high, for He Himself is kind to the ungrateful and the wicked. Be merciful, just as your father is merciful.

But, we need to ask, how does the prophet Jesus put his body where his mouth is in his ministry? He does so, Luke shows us, by placing himself at the disposal, not of the rich and powerful, but of the poor, the demon-possessed, the ill, women, children, all those regarded by the elite as not worthy of attention, much less service. Jesus touches, and is touched by, all those in his society whom others mock, insult, injure, and exclude, because they do not, in the eyes of the elite (whether political or religious or in combination) really matter.

Of all the ancient figures of whom we know, for example, Jesus is the only one who actually saw children as children, who carried them in his arms, who declared that the very measure of God's kingdom is the reception and care of children. This flies in the face of all we know: children are, economically speaking, the most obvious drags on adult self-preoccupation. They take and do not give back. They drain our resources without replenishing them. They sap adult energies that might have gone into building bridges or writing dissertations. Children are the least valuable assets in the portfolio of the elite. But what Jesus proclaims, he embodies: bring the little children to me.

As for loving those who hate you, Jesus repeatedly sits at table, not only with the sinners and tax collectors who seek to be with him, but as well with those among the religious elite, the very ones who reject his prophetic message, who hate, mock, insult, and seek to exclude him, and finally, as they did the prophets of old, kill him. We see how fearful a challenge it is to the presumption of the elite that the poor are to serve their needs for someone boldly to serve the needs of the lowly and outcast.

Now, as Jesus approaches Jerusalem, he is hailed by the "multitude of his disciples," the small band that had followed him from Galilee. They cry, "Blessed is the King who comes in the name of the Lord, peace in heaven and glory in the highest" (19:36).

But by entering Jerusalem, the prophet-king has put his body on the threshold of deadly danger. He is entering the place where all the kingdoms managed by Satan intermingle, the center of religious and political rule, the home of the establishment. The Pharisees, right on cue, demand of Jesus that he silence his disciples' glad cry. As throughout Luke's Gospel, the good news from God is not welcome to those who already have their comfort, who are already rich by the world's measure. Jesus tells them that if the disciples were silenced, then the very stones would cry out (19:40).

And as he gazes on the city, Jesus weeps over it, saying:

PUTTING THE BODY WHERE THE MOUTH IS

If this day you only knew what makes for peace—but now it is hidden from you. For the days are coming upon you when your enemies will raise a palisade against you; they will encircle you and hem you in on all sides. They will smash you to the ground and your children within you, and they will not leave one stone upon another within you because you did not recognize the time of your visitation (19:41–44).

Then, Luke has Jesus place his body in the place where his prophetic challenge to the world's kingdom would be most visible and most provocative: the magnificent temple, which was at once the most holy place and the most lucrative marketplace. "Then he entered the temple area and proceeded to drive out those who were selling things, saying, 'My Father's house should be a house of prayer, but you have made it a den of thieves'" (19:45–46). We remember—as perhaps some of those seeing him remembered—that, even as a boy, Jesus had caused a commotion in that same temple area, and had declared to his parents, "Why do you seek me? Do you not understand that I must be about my father's business?" (2:49).

The entire logic of Jesus's prophetic mission leads directly to this moment of protest against a kingdom run on the basis of merchandizing, in the name of a kingdom whose members pray with empty pockets, "Father, holy be your name; your kingdom come; give us each day our daily bread, and forgive us our sins, for we ourselves forgive everyone in debt to us. And do not subject us to the final testing" (11:2–4).

Jesus's action in the temple is only a gesture, just a prophetic gesture. He simply puts his body where his mouth is. It is like the young black students sitting at the all-white soda fountain at Walgreens in the 1950s. It's like a simple march across Selma bridge. It's like pouring blood over nuclear warheads. Just a gesture. But depending on where the body language is spoken, it can signify, it can arouse, it can even stir the beginnings of change.

For this reason, it is correctly perceived by the powers-that-be as a serious threat. Jesus's entry into the city as a prophet-king, and his putting his body where his mouth was in the capital of his enemies, ensured that he would, like prophets before and after him, need to be eliminated (11:47–50).

But we who gather still in his name and proclaim him as our Lord, we carry as etched in our hearts the words he spoke to his disciples at his last meal. Just when he was sharing the bread as his body given for them and the cup as the blood of a new covenant—in other words, just when Jesus was expressing both in speech and body the character of God's kingdom—his closest followers fell into an argument over who was to be the greatest among them! Jesus responds:

> The kings of the Gentiles lord it over them, and those in authority over them are called benefactors. But among you it shall not be so. Rather, let the greatest among you be as the youngest, and the leader as the servant. For who is the greater, the one who sits at table or the one who serves? Is it not the one who sits at table? Yet I am among you as the one who serves (22:24–27).

What then, can we who gather in the name of the prophetic king Jesus this Monday in Holy Week learn from Luke's portrayal of him?

In the book of Acts, Luke shows how the outpouring of the Holy Spirit on all flesh was to empower Jesus's followers to carry forward his prophetic mission.

His prophetic mission does not necessarily demand that each of us march or protest or go to jail. But it does demand of each of us that what we profess, we also put into practice, that we put our body where our mouth is. A start is to align ourselves more with those who are mocked and despised by the elite in our world than with the elite who are the chief mockers and despisers.

We might thereby learn from the poor what it truly means to be poor, from the grieving what grief truly means, from those who hunger how hunger can diminish human dignity, from those who are marked as different how stigma is a form of suffering. By simply associating ourselves with the youngest and weakest and least attractive among us we can act as members of the kingdom announced and embodied by our Lord Jesus. And we may even learn to love our enemies and to give without reward.

SPEAKING TRUTH IN FACE OF DECEIT[1]

Luke 20:1–8, 20–26

My sisters and brothers, we are reflecting on Luke's version of Jesus's last days. Both Luke and Matthew follow their common source Mark in having Jesus's prophetic act of cleansing the temple—an act they all agree was the precipitant for the plot among his opponents to seek his death—with a strangely lengthy interlude.

They portray Jesus as teaching daily in the temple to a crowd that hung upon his words and in the presence of those trying to figure out how to get rid of this populist prophet without turning the crowd against themselves, or causing the kind of riot for which Passover Jerusalem was notorious and which sometimes brought on savage reprisal from the occupying Roman garrison.

The scene is set by Luke immediately following Jesus's declaration that they had made his father's house of prayer into a den of thieves, by noting: "Every day he was teaching in the temple area. The chief priests, the scribes, and the leaders of the people, meanwhile, were seeking to put him to death, but they could find no way to accomplish their purpose because all the people were hanging on his words" (19:47–48). So, they fall back on the tried-and-true method of verbal entrapment. They can diminish and destroy this prophetic pretender by forcing him to "misspeak himself" as we would say it today.

This part of the Synoptic Gospels features a series of verbal encounters between Jesus and the leaders of various Jewish parties. They pose questions and Jesus responds, before he turns the tables on them with a question of his own, and with an attack on their economic corruption and oppression. The interlude ends with Jesus, still standing in its precincts, prophetically

---

1. Preached at All Saints Church in Atlanta Tuesday of Holy Week, 2019; the second of two.

announcing to his followers the fall of the temple—not a stone of it shall stand upon another—and the destruction of Jerusalem, accurately, as it turns out.

What narrative purpose is served by gathering this set of exchanges between Jesus and those hostile to him? For the earliest church, I think, it helped position Jesus among the various rival groups of first-century Judaism—scribes and Pharisees, Herodians, Sadducees—by having them pose questions typical of their sect and providing Jesus's response. For the evangelists, this cluster of exchanges provided dramatic spacing between Jesus's entry into the city and his subsequent arrest, trial, and execution, showing a steady intensification of the conflict between this back-country prophet and the powers that be, and a sense of the deep divide between the kingdom proclaimed by Jesus and the business-as-usual kingdom of this world.

For liturgically-minded Episcopalians, the interlude suggests what Jesus may have been doing between the time when he entered the city and disrupted the temple commerce, and the night he washed his disciples' feet. What was happening to him in other words, on Monday through Wednesday of Holy Week. For us today, it offers the opportunity to think about another aspect of Jesus's prophetic persona in Luke.

In my last presentation, I spoke about prophecy as putting one's body where one's mouth is, that is, putting profession into practice even at great risk. I suggested that Jesus's entry into the place of his enemies, and his occupation of the temple as his father's place of prayer embodied the reversal of human measures that was the good news from God he proclaimed.

But now, our imaginations are stretched to envisage the scene suggested by the evangelist: we must imagine the enormous space of the temple precincts. Think of an area roughly five football fields by five football fields. Imagine tens of thousands of pilgrims passing through with sacrificial animals. Picture a tiny corner of that great space occupied by Jesus and his followers that draws those seeking his teaching, draws as well the agents and scouts sent by the establishment to trap him—not simply for embarrassment, but for elimination.

This is not an idyllic spot by the Sea of Galilee. This is the big city, the home of government, of religion, of military force. This is where people get crucified. Mr. Smith has come to Washington and is standing on the steps of the capital, facing the cameras and the microphones. The analogy is not that farfetched. This set of exchanges, if played out dramatically, would resemble nothing so much as a press conference in contemporary politics. The sophisticated and savvy questioners are always in search of the "gotcha" moment that will bring down the populist pretender. Our interest today, then, is on another dimension of prophecy, how it means speaking the truth in the face of deceit. We cannot examine each of the exchanges in detail so I will focus on only two: the question concerning Jesus's authority and that concerning payment of taxes to Caesar. These exchanges above all show us the distinction between twisted and true speech.

Luke tells us that Jesus "was teaching the people in the temple area and proclaiming the good news" when a delegation made up of chief priests, scribes, and elders approach him. These are the elite of the Jewish people, the members of the Sanhedrin. They are our senators, congressman, congressional aids; or perhaps, our bishops and cardinals, members of the Vatican curia. As we would expect of such establishment types, their questions concern credentials: "Tell us by what authority are you doing these things, or who has given you authority?" He is on their turf and they have not authorized him, so he must be an interloper. Where are his bona fides, his Yeshiva diploma, his parade permit from the temple police?

Now remember the context. Jesus has driven out merchants from the area because a house of prayer had been made a den of thieves. His words recall those of prophet Daniel (Dan 7:11) but, their questions implies, a prophet needs a permit to be a prophet. And since they did not give him a permit, no one could have. Their question, therefore, is not really a question at all. It is a challenge and a threat. And it is a threat that is terribly revealing of their own assumption: the temple is not God's house of prayer, it is their property for profit. Worse than Jesus acting like he was Jeremiah is the fact that he threatens their own *exousia*—the same word for "authority" used by Satan when he tempted Jesus with *exousia* over all the kingdoms of the earth, "for they are mine to give" (Luke 4:6), and Jesus declared, "You shall worship the Lord your God; Him alone shall you serve" (Luke 4:8; Deut 6:13).

Jesus responds with a question of his own: "Tell me, was John's baptism of heavenly or of human origin?" It is such a simple question, yet it cuts sharply to the corruption adherent in their challenge. Prophets receive their authority from God, not from human institutions. Every Jew knows that. So what about Jesus's predecessor, John, who preached a baptism of repentance—and of economic reform? They are at once caught in their own duplicity.

And their reaction is that of all the deceitful: "They discussed this among themselves" (20:5). They went into a huddle. They consulted with each other. They sought a politically plausible narrative. They are not stupid; they understand the point of Jesus's question. If they say John's prophetic mission was from God, then why hadn't they believed him and repented? They clearly had no more recognized John as a prophet than they now recognize Jesus. But to say that John was sent by God would be to acknowledge an authority superseding their own. Prophets need no divinity degree.

But they grasp as well that they have fallen into a trap they had themselves devised. If they say that John's authority was of human origin, they are both lying—they knew as everyone knew that John had not attended Candler—and they expose their unbelief in God's authority before the people who recognized John as a prophet, the way they are now regarding Jesus as a prophet. Out of fear of the people, the boldness of the leaders deflates. They answer Jesus with the biggest lie possible: "We do not know from where it came" (20:7).

They knew alright, just as they knew where Jesus's authority came from. Their lie involves not their minds but their hearts. To acknowledge an *exousia* from God transcending their own is to cede their own *exousia* in the temple that is a house of prayer to the God who gives all *exousia*. Jesus closes the exchange with the simple declaration, "Neither shall I tell you by what authority I do these things" (20:8). The simplicity of prophetic speech reveals the tangled duplicity of speech that is not open to truth but only defends positions of power.

Luke then has Jesus turn from this exchange to address the people with the parable of the vineyard owner who has his emissaries rejected by the managers and finally has his beloved son killed by them, with the result that the owner takes away the vineyard from them and gives it to others. The leaders heard the parable, and "sought to lay hands on him at that very hour, but they feared the people, for they knew that he had spoken this parable against them" (20:19). So, they shift from direct to indirect entrapment which brings us to the exchange concerning payment of taxes to the emperor. This passage has been endlessly analyzed by those interested in the respective powers of pope and emperor, but my interest is only in what Luke shows us about speaking truth in the face of deceit.

Luke leaves the reader in no doubt concerning the duplicitous motivations and methods of Jesus's opponents. I want to render the Greek idiomatically here. The Sanhedrin leaders "had him under observation" or "under surveillance" (*paratērēsantes*). And they commissioned spies (*enkathētous*), who falsely presented themselves as honest (*hypokrinomenous dikaious einai*), precisely in order to trap him by his speech (*epilabontai autou logou*). And Luke gives us the purpose: "so that they might hand him over to the power and the authority of the governor"—that is, not the Jewish court, but the Roman prefect. We know that in the distant provinces of the empire, such prefects had the use *ius gladii*, the right to execute on the grounds of even the slightest quiver of revolutionary unrest. And we know that Pontius Pilate was not reluctant to exercise this option, especially at feasts like the Passover when the huge crowds in Jerusalem tended to seethe with resentment against the Roman occupation.

The secret agents' first words seems to compliment Jesus, but their flattery actually serves to set him up: "Teacher, we know that you speak and teach rightly, and you are not a respecter of persons—(that is, you are impartial and fair)—instead, you teach the way of God on the basis of truth" (20:21). They do not believe a single word of this. If they did, they would not accept the commission as secret agents and set out to get a prophet arrested for insurrection. They are only setting a trap from which they think there is no escape: "Is it lawful [or necessary] for us to pay tribute [or a tax] to Caesar or not?" (20:20).

The question seems to present the perfect no-win set of options. He is trapped, they think, between the Jews who equate true religion with national independence and the Jews who cooperate with the Roman authorities to preserve the ancient religious institutions. If Jesus says they should pay the tax, he will lose favor with those people who in the time of feasts are whipped with patriotic fervor. But if he says they should not pay the tax, he is exposed as a revolutionary before the vigilant Roman authority. Either answer brings him down.

The murderous malice of the simple-seeming question is neatly hidden by the flattery that precedes it. Surely an honest teacher like Jesus, who is no respecter of persons, will answer in a way that dooms him. The duplicity of those questioning Jesus is linked to their hypocrisy, for if they themselves had not been paying the tax, they would not be there to challenge this populist prophet. And they neatly suppress the fact that a major part of their financial resources is derived from trading in imperial and other coinage in the temple precincts.

Luke tells us that Jesus "recognized their craftiness/deceit (*panourgia*)," and asked them to show him the coin with which the tax was paid, and to identify the image and inscription on the coin. Whose were they? Caesar's. The emperor produced the coin which was the medium of tax payment. So, Jesus neatly sidestepped the impossible dilemma with the simple declaration, "Give to Caesar what is Caesar's." It's the emperor's coinage. He can demand it back. But then Jesus adds the phrase that turns their phony dilemma back on them, "Give to God what is God's."

Jesus simply rejects the false equivalence of religion with politics. They are, in truth, radically incommensurate. There is no political position that aligns perfectly with God's kingdom, and the rule of God is never expressed adequately by any political posture. Being a faithful Jew means worshiping the Lord God with all one's heart and all one's mind and all one's life. Such devotion can neither be abetted nor impeded by the one who imposes and collects taxes, no matter what he calls himself or is called by others. It is not an image on a coin that constitutes idolatry; it is a derangement of the will that mitigates the absolute demands of obedience to God with the relative advantages of expedience for the self.

Jesus's simple and clear distinction between true religion—giving back to God everything for everything comes as gift from God—and human politics—paying a ruler taxes as demanded—this simple and clear distinction only became muddled when Christianity fatefully wedded itself to imperial power with Constantine, and when popes claimed to govern Europe and not the life of the spirit. Thus, centuries of anguished exegesis. Thus, turning Jesus's simple speaking of truth in the face of deceit into another and even more complex form of deceit, namely, that of finding scriptural authority for human ambition.

I don't think this short reflection has distorted the meaning of Luke's text. But I hope that my plain reading of his text makes its contemporary relevance clear. We live in an age of "gotcha" discourse, whether in the traditional press and media or in blogs, Twitter, Instagram, and the other digital means of intemperate and thoughtless verbal expression. We may ourselves grow confused about the difference between speaking truth to power—the work of authentic prophecy—and distorting truth for the sake of power, even if the power is as lowly and despicable as that achieved by anonymous trolling. The letter of James tells us, "Be quick to hear, slow to speak, slow to anger, for human anger does not accomplish God's righteousness." If we look into our hearts and our own patterns of speech, we can see how far we fall short of this wisdom, and how much further short of the courageous simplicity of the prophet Jesus.

GOOD FRIDAY

PRAYER AND SUFFERING[1]

Hebrews 5:7–10
Mark 14:35–42

My sisters and brothers in Christ, before we light a new fire this year, or praise the Lord for his wondrous works, or sing the new song which is Halleluiah,
    Let us, for this moment together,
    On the day we remember the death our savior died for us,
Let us remember him who is the pioneer and perfecter of faith;
For the way he has gone is the way to which we are called,
And that way leads through death.
It is when we consider the death of Jesus that we discover the nature of faith that prayer expresses. It is when we consider the suffering of Jesus that we find what the prayer of faith involves.
But I do not wish to consider this today. I am too tired, for one thing, too filled with the care of littler, more immediate, preoccupying, anxious things. I hurt in ways I'd rather not discuss.
And so, I suspect, do you. Besides, prayer and suffering are tautologous, are they not? A little rest, please, for the weary, who have, with all these cares, "grown hard of hearing."
Besides, the link of prayer and suffering is obvious, but not helpful.
When I suffer, I pray all right, and feel foolish and craven when I do, saying, "I should have handled that one on my own," and "why didn't I pray when I was happy, when everyone said I was doing so well, and my tooth didn't ache in the middle of this endless night?" A shoddy performance, this flinching before the dark: shameful.

---

[1]. Marquand Chapel, Yale Divinity School, 1980.

GOOD FRIDAY

And when I pray, I suffer, all right. I am amazed, the times I really pray and not just yell, when I don't just shuffle the old slogans and pose the old postures, but
> Listen for, pay attention to, the silence
> Which builds so threateningly within me
> Where I sit
> With nothing happening
> And nothing likely to, either,
> Except more loneliness—

I am amazed, really, at the suffering that seeps from the scabs of yesterday's hurts that I thought healed or at least covered over with words, mine and theirs, and now, look, ripped open again by truth.
But this is what I don't understand:
> When I am suffering and pray, it is because I want to stop suffering.
> And when I am praying and start to suffer
>> Because of the way the word of truth
>> Insinuates itself
>> Into the silent spaces
>> Between the whirling wheels of my desires,
>> That word of truth posed in the silence
>> By the One who alone can pose it as question to me,
>> "Who are you, really?"
>
> Then I stop praying. I flee such suffering.

Who can pray in suffering and suffer through prayer? I can't.
Therefore, I must look to Jesus, who is the pioneer who said "yes" to his father,
And is perfecter because he said "yes" once for all, completely.
I look to Jesus and his faith expressed by prayer
Not because his faith expressed by prayer is like mine,
But because, by the gift of the Spirit given from his bloody side,
Mine might become progressively more like his.
And so, I look to him who, in the days of his flesh cried out with loud shouts to be saved from death. Jesus, too, wanted to live, wanted to live on his own terms and in his own way and in accord with his heart's desires; being human as we are, He had to have had such desires, such projects that were dear to him. And he shouts,
> "Father, let this cup pass from me.
> I do not want to drink it. Please!"

In this, Jesus is like me, and I am comforted.
But then, Hebrews reminds us, "He learned obedience from the things he suffered." And in the garden, I hear,
"My Father!
Not as I will, but as you will!"
Jesus, fixed in the longing of his heart for life, for self-definition, for his own way, was called to another's way,
And he allowed his father's will to enter the space of his loneliness and fear, unclasp his clutch on his own life, and say,
"Yes, my Father!"
In this, he is not like me, and I am challenged.
He is the one who in the long nights of silence learned to hear his Father's voice calling him out of his narrow vision into vistas too painful to glimpse, even for him, except partially, bit by bit. And every step of listening, of saying yes, was a step toward death and through death to new life, as he stepped beyond the space of human measure into the one measured by God alone, and became, progressively, obedient Son.
So Jesus, in prayer, learned suffering by his obedience, and obedience from the things he suffered.
Therefore, he whose first words on coming into the world were,
"Lo, I have come to do your will O Lord" (Heb 10:7)
Found the "yes" of prayer itself to be suffering.
Therefore, he who did not flee from the suffering of prayer
Found it freeing at last,
For the gesture of exquisite intimacy
In his transfixed open arms on the cross
And the utter simplicity of truth
In his anger and his pain.
Therefore, it is through him that we say "Amen" to the Father.

SIMPLE NOT EASY[1]

Isaiah 52:13—53:12
Hebrews 10:1–10
Luke 23:26–49

My sisters and brothers in Christ,
Not everything simple is easy.
Dying is simple, but rarely easy.
Simple like a conjuring trick,
        Hand faster than the eye
        Now you see me now you don't
        Here now gone now.
The ultimate vanishing act,
But done without props, sometimes,
Like naked on a tree exposed on a hill,
No strings but real nails.
It is the simplest thing, really.
It is done all the time.
On the evidence, it is the most consistent accomplishment
Of our species—dying.
We have worked variations on the theme,
It is true,
But the end is always the same
        The old soft shoe off stage
        The flick of the veil and gone.
So, why do we crawl to this musty cave

---

1. Preached at Yale's Battell Chapel, April 9, 1982. I was so frightened at speaking in this historical space that my preparations had completely stalled. I was paralyzed. Starting near Thursday midnight, in desperation I sat and wrote out this verse-form sermon in one frenzied spasm.

SIMPLE NOT EASY

In the middle of the city
At this unlikely hour
On this profane day
      While the wheels of traffic
      Whisper around the stone walls
      That the circles they spin
      Are more real—
Why do we come to contemplate another skull,
Another gallows,
Knowing so many already?
Surely we know the drill.
We have seen the
      Chessmen Gilmores
      Kennedys Kings
      Lincolns Gandhis
      Beckets,
Parade before us
In the noble documentary march
Orchestrated by bullets, swords, and clever chairs with many wires,
And have known
      The cancers cankers
      Tumors traumas
      Depressions defeats
      Of homelier crucifixions
Maybe our own, and if not, then surely in the pew beside us.
      Or we can think of those in cars outside these walls,
      Whispering in wheels around the city
      Carrying in blasted skulls
      The violence of a thousand worlds
      And feeling for a trigger.
Simple, yes, this dying,
Reducing complexity to dust;
And common, yes,
We do it all the time.
But easy?
No.
You would think with so much practice,
Our race would find it easy.

GOOD FRIDAY

But it is a trick each of us
Gets to do just once.
We'd better get it right.
Which is probably at least one of the reasons
We are here today at this odd time
To look back over a road we still have to travel,
To remind ourselves of what we have forgotten
About our future,
By looking to Jesus
And the way he died.
We have come together
To hear the story again,
Slowly,
To be sure we have it right.
In an act of great and thrilling imagination
    We pull our death into this room with us
        All the dying within and without us
        On this cruel April day
            When Falkland and Holy Land
            And every land and every hand
            Is stained with blood
            And every heart
                In mental ward
                Or violated bed
            Wants to cry to someone
            Save us! Save us!
    We pull all our death with us
    Into this suddenly crowded room
    And say to ourselves, listen!
        Where you are going
        He has been
        And he's the only one to come back alive
        So he must have done it right.
We know now
That we cannot escape the cold
That grips us even as we sit here
We cannot escape it
By reaching out our hands

SIMPLE NOT EASY

To the fire of self-deception
As Peter did last night in the courtyard; poor Peter, now so hungover with fatigue and grief
        Like us, the night after our betrayals
        Eyes now seared with pain;
Is he in that ragged line of those who have come as though to a spectacle, to see this new conjurer do the old trick, this time on a gibbet?
We know we cannot
Delay the reckoning
By spinning webs of
Philosophical; theological grace,
Draping them around our heads like altar lace,
Or by shouting
    Halleluiah!
    Christ is raised
Trying to get where he is now
Forgetting the way he had to go
    For the pronoun remains singular:
        He is raised
        But we are not,
        Not yet
            And still must go the way he went
            Without props
            With only X to mark the spot.
So we have come to listen
Not to recipes that make it easy
But stories that keep it simple;
    And as we listen
    We learn that what made it right
    The way Jesus did
    What we all dread
        This getting to be dead
    What made it right
    Was the way he gave himself to the job
    As though he was doing it by God
    For everyone
    As though this one time
    It had to be right.

GOOD FRIDAY

  Put his mind to it
  For once and for all
  Jesus did, this final
  Moment of discovery
When the one who sprang into life
With the glad cry, "I have come to do your will O Lord"
Found at the end
The ruthless logic
Of being a body
Driven home by the nails
  —being a body means in the end one way or another getting nailed—
Now said, "Yes father, I place my life in your hands."
Simple, yes?
But not easy.
  And so another text tells,
    "By that will we have been sanctified
    Through the offering of the blood
    Of Jesus Christ, once for all."
And the prophetic text which,
Looking to the suffering of the people,
Spoke of it as the death of a servant for all:
    So that something so simple a common
    As a lamb led to the slaughter
    Became a means of life for all
    And something so basic as getting it right
    Meant rightness for all:
    "By his knowledge shall the righteous one,
    My servant, make many to be accounted
    Righteous;
    And he shall bear their iniquities."
  So we can say now:
    "surely he has borne our griefs
    And carried our sorrows . . .
    With his stripes we are healed."
  Knowing that the servant foretold is Jesus,
  Who put his mind to the task once for all
  To do it right.

SIMPLE NOT EASY

He dies for all the ways we flee from death,
For all the ways we make others die in our place
For all the ways we choose the easy over the simple,
He dies.
And so we join those circling
The still silent pivot where Jesus hangs this hour
Hearing the voices shout
And wondering which is ours:
>We hear the voice of the leaders yelling,
>>"He saved others, let him save himself"
>As though that were the point.
>(They had never listened, of course);
>Jesus had told the old woman,
>>"Daughter your faith has saved you,"
>And told the father of the little dying girl,
>>"Don't fear. Only have faith and she shall be saved"
>Strange, if he had not followed his own advice.
>>And we hear the soldiers, those professional dealers in death,
yell:
>>"Save yourself if you are the king"
>Knowing as they do only one kind of power.
>And we hear the man hanged with him yell,
>>"Are you not the Christ? Save yourself and us."
Ah, this is the line we have been waiting for:
If you are the Christ, save yourself . . .
And us.
>Which is really the point of it all, right?
>What good is it having a savior
>If he doesn't save you
>From the only thing that counts?
With this forthright brigand
We too want to know
What is in Jesus's death for us,
How can it make something simple easy?
And so we must listen closely
To that other thief riveted to a cross
>Who observes that they were doing
>What came naturally,

GOOD FRIDAY

But Jesus was doing it the hard way:
    Being in the form of God
    And emptied out
    Being without sin
    And made sin
    Being made a curse
    By God's own word
And so he said to Jesus, simply,
    "Remember me."
And finally, we have come to hear
The last words of Jesus
Which summarize all his life
And tell us all we need to know
About conjuring:
    "Father, into your hands I commit my spirit."
Which is a simple thing to say
But not easy.
We have come to praise the God
Who gave himself to us in a son
    Who died with us to teach us how
Who gave us of his spirit
    So that we too can say with Jesus,
        "Father, into your hands, we commit our lives"
And we have come to say to Jesus,
    "Remember us, Lord, as we remember you."

REVELATORY DEATH[1]

Matthew 27:45–50

From noon onward, darkness came over the whole land until three in the afternoon. And about three o'clock, Jesus cried out in a loud voice, *Eli, Eli, Lama Sabachtani*, which means, "My God, my God, why have you forsaken me?" Some of the bystanders who heard it said, "This one is calling for Elijah." Immediately one of them ran to get a sponge; he soaked it in wine, and putting it on a reed, gave it to him to drink. But the rest said, "Wait, let us see if Elijah comes to save him." But Jesus cried out again in a loud voice, and gave up his spirit.

My brothers and sisters in Christ, like other ancient biographers of great people, the evangelists were eager to record Jesus's last words. The words spoken by a dying person were thought to reveal their true character. Recording them could offer an example to their followers.

Oddly, the four evangelists have Jesus saying different things at the moment of his death. Or, perhaps not oddly. The evangelists were not after all present at Jesus's death. They had no written notes. They needed to supply the words that best fit their understanding of Jesus's character.

John has Jesus declare, "It is finished," as he hands over his spirit. This is appropriate for the Jesus in John's Gospel who knows he is God's supreme self-revelation. Luke places in the mouth of Jesus the words of Ps 31:6, "Father, into your hands I commit my spirit." This is appropriate to Luke's Jesus, who is always at prayer and even at the end forgives his executioners. Both Mark and Matthew have Jesus say the last words I just read. They provide the Aramaic (Matthew puts the first two words in Hebrew) *Eli Eli Lama Sabachtani*, and its translation, "My God, my God, why have you

1. Reflection at Tre Ore service at the Basilica of the Sacred Heart in Atlanta, 2008.

forsaken—or abandoned—me?" The fact that Jesus here speaks in Aramaic makes some people think that these are probably the words that Jesus actually spoke. That's possible. But it is just as likely that Mark (and his editor Matthew) supplied this line in the same way that Luke and John supplied theirs, as a way of showing Jesus's character.

But what are we to learn of Jesus's character from these last words? They are, in truth, easily misunderstood. Mark and Matthew show us the first misunderstanding, when the bystanders, apparently not hearing the whole line, and identify *Eli* ("my God") as the name of the prophet Elijah (*Eli-Yah* = the Lord is God). We remember the tradition reported in Matt 17:10–12 that Elijah was to come before the Son of Man was revealed. These bystanders stop the man who tries to give Jesus wine to ease his pain—they are curious to see if Elijah will come. An interesting comment on *their* character.

Celsus, the late-second-century critic of Christianity, used the statement as evidence that Jesus could not have been God's son. His own words declared him as abandoned by God! Even some Christian theologians have taken these words in isolation as expressing Jesus's human experience of abandonment by God and of separation from the Father.

These are all misunderstandings, because, like the bystanders at the cross, such interpreters fail to recognize that the words, "My God, my God, why have you forsaken me" are the first words of Ps 22, which are meant to suggest all the other words of the psalm.

There are two things, then, that we learn about Jesus from these last words on the cross.

The first is that Jesus dies while praying. He therefore remains faithful to God until the end. He does, to be sure, experience his death as a kind of abandonment or forsakenness. A violent execution at the hands of the wicked challenges easy notions of how faithful people die peacefully in their beds. But Jesus does not turn away from God, even if he feels God has turned from him. He cries out to God in the most personal way possible: *My* God, *my* God, why have you forsaken *me*? Jesus does not cry out to his executioners for mercy or to his friends for comfort. He cries out to the One whose will be came into the world to do, and he exposes to his Father all the pain he feels. This is the truest of prayers, for prayer is essentially being true in the presence of God.

The second thing we learn about Jesus's character comes from the realization that the evangelists Mark and Matthew supply the first line of

Ps 22 as a way of alerting readers to the entire psalm, knowing that as one who constantly prayed the psalms, Jesus would have known and intended all that is suggested by that first line.

The psalm alternates the painful experience of the righteous one who is attacked by others despite his innocence, and declarations of confidence in the God who saves.

The words of misery are strong and correspond perfectly to Jesus's suffering: "I am a worm and hardly human, scorned by everyone, despised by the people; they mock me, 'You relied on the Lord, let Him rescue him.'" And again, "Like water my life drains away, all my bones grow soft . . . as dry as potsherd is my throat, my tongue sticks to my palate, you lay me in the dust of death"; and again, "So wasted are my hands and feet that I can count all my bones. They stare at me and gloat; they divide my garments among them, for my clothing the cast lots."

Equally strong, and equally true, though, are the words of confidence spoken by the psalm, confidence not in the self, but in "the one enthroned as the Holy One, in whom our ancestors trusted; they trusted you and you rescued them; to you they cried out and they escaped; in you they trusted and were not disappointed." The psalm records the particular closeness with God that was Jesus's: "You drew me forth from the womb, made me safe at my mother's breast. Upon you I was thrust from the womb, from birth you are my God." On this basis, he says, "Do not stay far from me, for trouble is near, and there is no one to help . . . you Lord, do not stay far off; my strength, come quickly to help me . . . save me from the lion's mouth, my poor life from the horns of wild bulls."

At the end of the psalm, this confidence shifts in time. The psalmist pictures a future in which he stands in the midst of the assembly praising God for the way "in which [God] did not turn away from me but heard me when I cried out." He imagines how "all the ends of the earth will worship and turn to the Lord, all the families of nations will bow before you, for kingship belongs to the Lord, the ruler over all the nations." And then, this startling declaration, in which the early church, like the evangelist, saw the suffering and death of Jesus as leading to his exaltation: "All who sleep in the earth will bow low before God, all who have gone down into the dust will kneel in homage. And I will live for the Lord, my descendants will serve you."

Jesus's last words in Matthew's Gospel are words of prayer. They do not express despair because of his suffering, but the most profound hope in the

GOOD FRIDAY

God who calls into being that which is not, and gives life to the dead. His words instruct us in how to die, and how to live.

THE SUFFERING SERVANT[1]

Matthew 27:40–43

My sisters and brothers in Christ, the passion accounts are written by witnesses to an execution of a Jew carried out by Roman soldiers in first-century Palestine. They are not eyewitness accounts. They do not provide a confused and sketchy report of something seen in the blur of daily activity.

Neither are they like snapshots of a crime scene. They are more like portraits that have been painted and repainted over the years, with each layer representing another stage of discovery and appreciation. Portraits differ from photographs in the depth of their interpretation.

The self-portraits of Rembrandt bear witness to his life at each of its stages, but they do so less by providing a precise picture than by expressing the artist's deepest levels of interpretation, not of his face but of his life. Gazing at portraits gives us insight into a subject's character but also invites insight about ourselves.

The four Gospels are like such portraits. They witness to the death of Jesus by the way they interpret it. The way the Gospels converge on the main points lends weight to their credibility concerning the central facts of the event of Jesus's execution. The way they differ in detail gives depth to the meaning of the event. Paying attention to their distinctive portraits of Jesus gives us insight into his character and also invites us to insight about our own.

We hear the respective passion narratives best when we hear them in connection with the overall portrait of Jesus in each Gospel, because the character Jesus displays at his death is already demonstrated in his life. Reading this way also helps us connect the story of Jesus's death to our

[1]. Reflection at the Tre Ore service on Good Friday at the Basilica of the Sacred Heart, Atlanta, 2009.

story. We will not all be crucified. But we will all suffer and die. And the way we are in our lives now will almost surely be the way we will be in our final moments. Character is not easily changed.

The link between the manner of Jesus's death and the manner of his life can be seen in Matthew's emphasis on the title "Son of God" in his portrayal of Jesus's crucifixion.

The leaders and the people pass by the place of execution and revile Jesus. They say, "You who would destroy the temple and rebuild it in three days, save yourself; if you are the son of God, come down from the cross" (27:40). Then they say, "Let him come down from the cross now, and we will believe in him. He trusted in God; let God deliver him now if he wants him, for he said, 'I am son of God'" (27:43).

This taunting of Jesus as God's Son hauntingly evokes Matthew's account of Jesus's temptation by the devil after his baptism. The people's cries echo Satan's voice when he challenges Jesus in the wilderness, "If you are the Son of God, command that these stones become loaves of bread," and, "If you are the Son of God, throw yourself down." And we remember Jesus's voice saying, "One does not live by bread alone but by every word that comes from the mouth of God," and "You shall not put the Lord God to the test," and "The Lord your God shall you worship; him alone you shall serve" (Matt 4:4–10).

Let us notice especially that last word, "serve." In Matthew's Gospel, Jesus is not God's Son as a divine victor untouched by human suffering, but rather as a servant—even a slave—who suffers the human condition fully in faithful obedience to God. Like the Gospel of Mark, Matthew understands Jesus in terms of the suffering servant depicted by the prophet Isaiah (52–53). When he has Jesus declare of himself, "The Son of Man did not come to be served but to serve and to give his life as a ransom for many" (20:27), he uses the language of Isaiah.

Indeed, Matthew expands this understanding of Jesus in his depiction of Jesus's ministry. He twice cites passages from the servant-songs of Isaiah to characterize Jesus's deeds. In Matt 8:17, he comments on Jesus's healing of the sick, "This was to fulfill the saying of the prophet, 'He took our infirmities and bore our diseases,'" directly quoting Isa 53:4. And in Matt 12:18–21, he provides a long citation from Isa 42:1–2, again with reference to Jesus's healings:

> Behold my servant whom I have chosen, my beloved, with whom I am well pleased. I will put my spirit upon him and he shall

THE SUFFERING SERVANT

proclaim justice to the nations. He will not wrangle or cry aloud nor will anyone hear his voice in the streets. He will not break a bruised reed or quench a smoldering wick, until he brings justice to victory and in his name will the nations hope.

When we come to Matthew's portrayal of Jesus's last days, then, we are schooled to recognize in his gestures and words the character of God's suffering servant. He seeks not his own will but the will of his Father (Matt 26:39, 42). He breaks bread for his followers and says, "Take and eat, this is my body," and gives them a cup, saying, "Drink from it, all of you, for this is my blood of the covenant, which will be shed for many for the forgiveness of sins" (Matt 26:26–28). We recognize in this Jesus the servant of whom the prophet said, "He gives his life as an offering for sin . . . and the will of the Lord shall be accomplished through him" (Isa 53:10).

The term "servant" suggests someone who willingly provides for others, and part of this positive image certainly derives from Jesus himself. But we must on this day also remember that the term servant also means in the original languages of the Bible a "slave," that is, one who is owned by another and serves at the beck and call of another. We must remember as well that slavery was a widespread phenomenon in the Roman Empire. It was not based on race, as was the slavery in antebellum America, but it was no less harsh. People became slaves because of financial loss, because of war, or simply because they found themselves unable to survive any other way. However they got to that state, once there, slaves were not persons but property. They could be bought and sold without any regard to their own desires. They could be put to death for the most trivial or even imaginary offenses, at the whim of their owners. To be a slave meant being outside the realm of human concern or protection.

Not coincidentally, Rome's preferred mode of extreme punishment for slaves—and those it wished to shame as though they were slaves—was crucifixion. This grisly combination of torture and slow asphyxiation was intended to make a point about Rome's absolute power over those it owned, whether slaves or subject peoples. Those killed in this fashion were exposed publicly to the gaze of all, denuded of power, of possessions, of self-control, of dignity. In a world that considered honor the greatest of human goods, crucifixion was the most shameful of all deaths.

When Matthew shows us the Son of God killed by crucifixion, he shows us how completely God has identified with the most rejected and reviled among humans.

GOOD FRIDAY

It is natural for us to ask how we might honor the one who has experienced such shameful suffering for us. Jesus himself told us as straightforwardly as possible in Matthew's Gospel how he wants to be honored.

It is not by giving him lofty titles but by living in the way he did. He tells his disciples, "Not everyone who says to me Lord, Lord, will enter the kingdom of heaven, but only the one who does the will of my father" (7:21). In Matthew's great scene of the final judgment (25:31–46), which pictures Jesus judging humans on the basis of their deeds, we find out what that will of the father is: as Jesus became servant to the little ones, and in his death absolutely identified with those who were slaves, so are Jesus's followers to treat their fellow humans, above all, the little ones.

The measure is simple: the way disciples treat those viewed by the world as not deserving honor is the way they treat Jesus. Jesus says, "I was hungry and you gave me food; I was thirsty and you gave me to drink; I was a stranger and you welcomed me; naked, and you clothed me; ill, and you cared for me; in prison and you visited me." They ask when they did these things—for none of us can literally see Jesus in the people we live with every day—Jesus answers, "Whatever you did for one of these least brothers of mine, you did for me."

We don't have to see Jesus, we need only see, and serve the needs of the little ones: the hungry, thirsty, naked, homeless, ill, imprisoned—all those who experience, all around us, the things Jesus experienced as a slave on the cross.

The parish of the Sacred Heart of Jesus can rightly rejoice in the ways in which it seeks to honor Jesus by serving the little ones in Atlanta and in Haiti: many among us have visited those in prison; collected food for the hungry and clothing for the naked; cared for those stricken with AIDS; worked to build houses for the homeless. These are indeed the marks of genuine discipleship, of learning from Jesus.

I wonder, though, if the little ones might not include many not listed by Jesus. I wonder, in fact, if the little ones here in our city of Atlanta might not include some who fall into the category of slaves. I wonder if our call to follow Jesus does not require of each of us that we examine carefully the ways in which we treat them.

We don't like to think that we still have slavery or indentured servitude in our advanced world. Yet we do, most obviously in those in our city caught in the web of drugs and sexual predation. But less obviously, we can look around us and see all the ways in which our busy lives are enabled, not simply by technology, but by the hard work—and often the trapped lives—of other human beings, who are truly "little ones" that too often neither we nor anyone else really sees them: think of the bus drivers and check-out clerks and stockers at Walmart and Kroger, the waiters and busboys at restaurants, the dishwashers and house cleaners and gardeners and sanitation people, the single-parent secretaries and staff people at the DMV and VA and phone company and airport, that make our life in this city possible.

Do we even see them as people with families and stories like our own, with sufferings as great as or even greater than our own, with dreams and talents as powerful as ours, yet, unlike ours, with no hope of fulfillment?

And if we do see them, do we treat them with respect and kindness and genuine interest? Do we seek to know them and honor them as those who bear our burdens, often without our awareness or recognition? Or do we despise them, treating them with way ancient Romans treated their slaves? Do we crucify the Lord Jesus by despising the very ones with which he identifies himself and whose shame and suffering he carried for our sake? I need to ask myself this question. Perhaps we all need to ask ourselves this question.

THE BODY LANGUAGE OF LOVE[1]

John 19:23–27

My brothers and sisters in Christ, as in the other Gospels, John's account of Jesus's death combines three elements. The first is the hard memory of Jesus's execution under state authority—crucifixion was the most shameful death in antiquity, one reserved for slaves and rebels, intended to humiliate as well as inflict the most exquisite torture before death.

The second is the interpretation of Jesus's death through the reading and rereading of Scripture, so that his death appears not as appropriate punishment for a false messiah or rebel against authority but as the ultimate act of love that God shows humans through the self-giving of his Son.

The third is the perspective of faith enlivened by the experience of resurrection—the presence of the paraclete-spirit that Jesus promised his followers just before his death would lead them into a greater understanding of who he was and what God was doing through him.

Thousands of years after John portrayed Jesus's death, then, we read today as this account was intended to be read: from the perspective of our own experience of the resurrection-spirit that Jesus has breathed on us, and with an appreciation for the depth of the description provided by John's use of Scripture.

But what of death itself? We don't come together like this on Good Friday to consider Jesus either as critical historians or as weepy sentimentalists. We come together to hear John's words as disciples, as students, who seek to learn more fully the character of the gift that God gave us by entering so fully into our humanity as to share even the most humiliating death.

We come as well to learn more fully the meaning of discipleship. We seek to learn how to follow Jesus in the way he had gone.

1. Reflection at the Tre Ore service, Basilica of the Sacred Heart, 2010.

THE BODY LANGUAGE OF LOVE

Sitting with his disciples at his last meal with them the night before his death, Jesus told them plainly what it meant to be his follower. He said he left them a new commandment by which all people could tell that they were his disciples. They are to love one another (14:34).

This is, in fact, the only commandment in John's entire Gospel. John has no Sermon on the Mount (such as we find in Matthew) or Sermon on the Plain (such as we find in Luke). John has no teachings on prayer or the sharing of possessions like the ones found in Luke. There is only this single, simple, commandment of mutual love. We are tempted by this, perhaps, to feel relieved, tempted perhaps to think that John makes it easier on us, that simple means easy.

We know all about love, we think. It comes to us naturally. Being a disciple of Jesus must mean simply being nice to each other, pleasant, tolerant, forgiving, even friendly, even generous. It means giving to each other out of our abundance, and taking from each other our fair share.

But then we notice that Jesus has not commanded us to love each other according to our own norms. People can recognize us as Jesus's disciples only if we love each other in the way Jesus loved us. "As I have loved you, so should you also love one another." Imitating the way Jesus has loved us means not looking at what comes naturally and calling that love. It means looking carefully at Jesus and learning what authentic love entails. And this changes everything.

Just before stating this command, in fact, Jesus gave a demonstration of what his sort of love means. He took off his outer garments and wrapped a towel around his waist and washed the feet of those at the table with him. He washed the feet not only of those who loved him, but also the feet of the enemy who had already determined to betray him. "Do you realize what I have done for you?" he asks them, "You call me 'teacher' and 'master,' and rightly so, for indeed I am. If I, therefore, the master and teacher, have washed your feet, you ought to wash one another's feet. I have given you a model to follow, so that as I have done for you, you also should do" (13:12–15).

The love that Jesus shows them does not consist in fine thoughts or splendid words or even deep sentiments. It is not a matter of head or heart at all. It is a matter of the body. It is a matter of service. It is a matter of doing the homeliest and smallest things for others, as others need them, not according to what we think or feel.

GOOD FRIDAY

Many among us in fact have learned the body language of love from Jesus. Moment by moment, moved by his spirit, we seek to serve in just this way. We bear with one another's burdens. We carry each other's loads. We scrub the pots after others have eaten and wash the clothes others have worn, and touch the places of pain in each other's bodies and minds.

But sometimes in the midst of such servant-love, we understandably grow weary, perhaps even depressed, perhaps even angry. We ask how long we must serve in this way and what such service might actually mean. The pots and clothes get dirty again, the burdens reappear with numbing consistency, the pain is never completely relieved. How can we keep going? Why should we keep going? Feet always need washing and they always get dirty again.

These are appropriate questions for us to ask as we contemplate the death of Jesus as John describes it. Four elements in his account may help our thinking our way to some answers.

First, in John's Gospel, Jesus is not abandoned at his death, in contrast to the other Gospels, which show Jesus's followers scattering and Jesus left all alone. In John, Jesus can see from his place of execution four women, including his mother, and the disciple whom he particularly loved. We might want to think, "How nice for him to have his family and friends with him as he dies." But then we realize, if he can see them, they can also see him: stripped naked, beaten, crowned with thorns, and slowly asphyxiating as his ability to breathe is suppressed by his weight hanging from the cross. His pain can only be increased by their pain, as they see him exposed to the crowd in this most shameful condition.

So how does Jesus wash their feet, even in his extremity? He sees to the need they will have at his imminent absence. To his mother he says, "Woman, behold your son," which has a deliberate ambiguity: "You see me as I am leaving; turn your gaze to the one beside you." And to make the meaning clearer, he says to his beloved disciple, "Behold, your mother." At the very end, he thinks of their need rather than his own.

Second, John tells us that, just before he dies, Jesus says, "I thirst." The full significance of this statement will become clear in a moment, but we notice that when Jesus has drunk from the wine extended to him, he says, "It is finished," and bowing his head, he hands over his spirit. He does not give up his spirit, he hands it over. John states this carefully. The one who thirsts still gives.

Third, John makes an explicit point of witnessing to the fact that when Jesus, already dead, did not have his legs broken—a common technique to speed the death by disabling the executed to raise himself to breathe—but instead, had his side pierced by a soldier's spear, and when pierced, blood and water flowed out of his side. Why such attention to such a seemingly small physiological detail?

Finally, John uses two verses from Scripture to interpret the meaning of these small details. When he cites "not a bone of it shall be broken" (Exod 14:26; Num 9:12), he points to Jesus as the Passover lamb, and we remember how John the Baptist cried out when he saw Jesus, "Behold the lamb of God who bears the sins of the world" (John 1:29). Jesus bears the burdens of others to the very end.

Then John cites an obscure line from the prophet Zechariah, "They shall look upon him whom they have pierced" (Zech 12:10). We can only grasp why John has quoted this line when we read the verse in its entirety: "I will pour out on the house of David and on the inhabitants of Jerusalem a spirit of grace and petition, and they shall look on him whom they have pierced, and they shall mourn for him as one mourns for an only son, and they shall grieve for him as one grieves over a firstborn." The blood and water from Jesus's side symbolize the outpouring of the Spirit that comes on us because of his death and resurrection.

John had signaled such a connection earlier in his Gospel, when he has Jesus cry out during the feast of Booths, "Let everyone who thirsts come to me and drink, the one who believes in me." As Scripture says, "Rivers of living water will flow from within him"(see Zech 14:8). John explains to the reader, "He said this with reference to the Spirit that those who came to believe in him were to receive. There was, of course, no Spirit yet, because Jesus had yet to the glorified" (John 7:37–39).

The fountain of the Holy Spirit that come from the side of the one who thirsts tells us how we have the strength to love as Jesus did. The strength is not ours. We are able to keep going because he lives within us and strengthens us beyond our own capacity.

We are called to this sort of servant-love, because it is the mysterious way in which God brings life to the world. To be disciples of Jesus means to live according to this same pattern. Jesus declared before his final hours:

> The hour has come for the son of Man to be glorified. Amen, amen, I say to you, unless a grain of wheat fall into the ground and die, it remains just a grain of wheat. But if it dies, it produces

much fruit. Whoever loves his life loses it, and whoever hates his life in this world will preserve it for eternal life. Whoever serves me must follow me, and where I am there also will my servant be. The Father will honor whoever serves me (12:23–26).

EASTER TO CHRIST THE KING

THE DAY OF RESURRECTION[1]

Psalm 118:24
John 20:1–18
1 Corinthians 5:7–8

My sisters and brothers in Christ, Scripture declares: "This is the day that the Lord has made; let us rejoice and be glad in it." *This* is the day, the day of resurrection, for Christians the holiest of days, the center of our very existence, the cause of our gathering in Jesus's name.

This is the day, today: we declare by our presence here that resurrection is not only something that happened to someone else long ago in the past. Resurrection is a reality that continues to touch and transform us today and every day. The resurrection of Jesus means above all that the one whose suffering and death we have so closely followed during the time of Lent, and have ritually enacted during the sacred triduum, has entered into God's life, has become life-giving Spirit who renews the face of the earth.

This is the *Day*, on which God's triumphant power over, within, and through creation is asserted against the destructive forces of sin and death, turning the long and sad night of human alienation into the possibility of human reconciliation. Jesus, God's Son, has been raised, and for us has become the sun of a new creation, whose radiance illumines and warms our lives.

This is the day *the Lord has made*. This eschatological day, this new creation day, is not one any human could accomplish. Beat with our wings as we might against the cage of death, we can never by our own strength break through. Wrestle grimly within the chains of sin as we might, we cannot by our own strength be unshackled. Only the one who first calls into existence that which is not has might enough for this, has a love sufficiently powerful to be caged in our mortal flesh and weighted with our

---

1. Preached at Cannon Chapel, Candler School of Theology, Easter 1996.

sinful chains, and then leap from the spiced tomb, casting aside all mortal cover, all sinful weight, and fly—not away from us, no, but through the winged Spirit into a new closeness, a more profound intimacy with us, so that though not yet altogether free from mesh or lightened of mail, we also can hope one morning to fly, and can even now move more blithely through our groundling intimations and imitations of flight.

Let us *rejoice* and *be glad* in it. As at our beginning, so now; as now, so at our beginning. We rejoice in the power of God that so suffuses the human body of Jesus that he becomes "life-giving Spirit" (1 Cor 15:45). We rejoice in the gift of that same Spirit in our own bodies, in the flame that this rising sun has flung upon the earth, and in whose light, at last, we can see light, and so see all else new as well.

When we grasp that the resurrection means not the resuscitation of a corpse but the transfiguration of mortal flesh into glorified body, when we recognize that as it is now, so was it at the beginning, then we can begin to understand the puzzling stories told of the first experiences of the risen Lord among his followers.

These stories, such as the ones we have read this morning—Mary's visit to the tomb, the disciples' footrace, Mary's conversation with the man she thinks is a gardener—these stories are notoriously ill-suited to the purposes of history. All four Gospels have empty-tomb stories, for example, but each version involves different visitors, different encounters, different messages, and different responses. Three of the Gospels also tell stories of encounters that followers have with Jesus. But these stories likewise involve different people, different places, and different results.

The stories cannot be harmonized or arranged into a satisfactory chronological sequence. Indeed, they resist history altogether.

For this very reason, they are most precious, most true, for they point to the fundamental mystery of the resurrection. The Jesus whom other humans now encounter is continuous with the earthly Jesus but is also discontinuous—in order to be present to all human bodies, the Spirit of Jesus must necessarily transcend (without abandoning) his individual body. To use language completely inadequate to the task, the resurrected Jesus is available to be encountered by others in time and space precisely because he is no longer himself defined by time and space.

The stories we read this morning, then, like all the resurrection accounts, are based on real human experiences of the past; we remember how

THE DAY OF RESURRECTION

Paul in 1 Cor 15:3–8, provides a list of some who "had seen the Lord," many of them still around in his day.

But like all the resurrection stories, these are also fashioned in light of the continuing experience of Jesus in the church and seek to express not only what happened back then but also what continues to happen now. What a heavy burden, what an impossible load for narratives to bear! Yet because they accept that burden, these stories are radiant with the light they struggle to contain, and speak to us today the truth of the resurrection: Jesus is the same yet different; Jesus is absent yet more present than ever; Jesus is unmistakably himself yet can appear to anyone we might meet in a garden or on the road; Jesus cannot be grasped yet calls us by our personal name; Jesus is not simply a man we once knew but is now and forever "Rabbouni," my master.

It is in the light of Jesus's resurrection that we correctly perceive his earthly ministry. Jesus is not simply a peasant or poet or agrarian reformer or trader in quips. He is, as Peter rightly stated to the household of Cornelius, the Word God sent to Israel preaching the good news of peace, the One anointed by God with the Holy Spirit and power, which led him to go about doing good and healing all those oppressed by the devil (Acts 10:38–46). In short, we perceive the ministry of Jesus itself as God's work in the world to transform, not the accidental arrangements of society but the fundamental structures of human existence.

It is in the light of the resurrection that we, like the first believers, reread Torah and find in Ps 118 not merely the resurrection verses with which this sermon began, but also the essential script of the messianic drama: "The stone which the builders rejected has become the cornerstone; this is the Lord's doing: it is marvelous in our eyes" (Ps 118:22). And seeing Jesus as the shunned and shattered stone that God uses to build a new temple in the Spirit also enables us to see all the scorned stuff of creation, all the bits and pieces we so easily dismiss, all the fragmented and broken bodies, all the shattered and shuttered hearts and minds, in a new and perhaps more cautious and perhaps more hopeful light; certainly, we cannot ever view any broken stones in quite the same way.

It is in the light of the resurrection, finally, that we are called to view our own lives in an entirely new way. The truth of the resurrection is not confirmed or disconfirmed by the analysis of ancient texts or the exhumation of ancient bones, but by the presence or absence of transformed lives among those who proclaim Jesus as Lord. "Christ our Paschal Lamb," says

Paul, "has been sacrificed; let us, therefore, celebrate the festival, not with the old leaven, the leaven of malice and evil, but with the unleavened bread of sincerity and truth" (1 Cor 5:7–8).

My sisters and brothers, the only convincing sign of the resurrection in our world is the transformed lives of those who confess the resurrection. If we do not live as though in a new creation, why should anyone find the claim of a new creation credible?

If we do not bring a word of peace to our world, work for the healing of the sick, struggle to lift the burdens of those afflicted by all the demons for whom contemporary culture provides such a rich breeding ground, do we not become incredible, even to ourselves, and our sounds of rejoicing empty and embarrassing?

If we do not put aside the old leaven of malice and evil to speak and act in sincerity and truth, do we not discredit our risen Lord, do we not diminish the truth we have gathered here today to proclaim?

PARADOXICAL LIFE[1]

1 John 1:1—2:2
John 20:19–31

My sisters and brothers in Christ, to be Christian means having a high tolerance for paradox. The British essayist G. K. Chesterton once said that paradox is truth calling attention to itself by standing on its head. He called it the logic of topsy-turvydom.

Chesterton gives the example of the young nobleman Francis who lived in the Italian city of Assisi. One day he stood on his head and suddenly saw his native city, not as a strong fortress reaching into the sky, but as a fragile bauble dangerously dangling over a blue abyss. In this topsy-turvy moment, Francis for the first time saw his city truly, for he saw it as contingent, suspended over nothingness. Francis popped to his feet, shed his rich clothes, and began a life of radical poverty. If the truth of things is the non-necessity of things, if the deepest reality is that all is free gift from God, then why not live that way? Francis would have been more of a paradoxical figure only if, having once spotted that truth, he had continued to live in Assisi exactly as he had before, dwelling in his town now as a bauble and not as a fortress.

Something in us, though, wants to be all way or all the other. If life is not permanent, then let's end it now. If I can't be a world-class pianist, don't get me started on piano lessons. If our relationship might end, why start it? If our city can't be strong and self-sufficient, why invest in its protection? If our children can't be perfect, why give them birth? This tendency to be all or nothing makes chronic illness the hardest of our afflictions—we're not well, and we're not desperately ill. Either make me an Olympic sprinter, or

---

1. Preached at Shandon Memorial Presbyterian Church, Columbia, South Carolina, first Sunday after Easter, 2000.

put me in a wheelchair; don't leave me here with intermittent and baffling shortness of breath.

Welcome to the world of paradox, which is the world of mystery, in which, heaven help us, you and I must dwell as those who invoke the name of Jesus as the risen Lord. It is the world in which we get to decide everyday whether the glass is half-full or half-empty, whether we are dying or rising to new life. It is a world for which we are constitutionally unfit. We are day people. We are night people. Give us no dusk, take away the dawn. Transport us direct from Christmas to July 4 and leave out all the sopping gray months between them.

When things are definite, we know where we are, who we are, and how to act. We don't have to decide what is what. We don't have to think so much, pay such close attention.

Why, we ask, does a God whom today's first reading declares as entirely light seem to deal so much in shadows?

If the God of light has created this world of ours, why isn't it shot through with radiance? Why are there blots of sickness and injury and violence and ignorance that argue for a blinder or more malicious or more capricious power at work? Why is there so much around us that screams there is no god, or at least not one who is both all-powerful and all good? How can we grasp that the blots can be seen at all only because of the light by which we see light?

Is this divine delicacy or a demure deceit, this dance of God behind the veil of appearances, forcing us to choose whether we dwell in an empty shall of delusion or a vessel full of transforming grace? How subtle of God to be everywhere in creation yet nowhere visible. How difficult is this freedom with which God has gifted us, so that we might by faith construe our world as one in which we constantly if obliquely encounter God's presence, but may also by lack of faith construe it as a dismal dog-run in which we never meet anything but our own fantasies.

As with creation, so also with the resurrection of Jesus that we celebrate the week after Easter. If Jesus were a good man who died a noble death and stayed dead, then we could get on with things. We could learn a few things from him as we have learned a few things from Socrates, but Jesus would demand no more of our attention than does Socrates. And if Jesus's resurrection were really eschatological in a world-ending spectacular fashion, if his inauguration of God's rule were really one that commanded every knee in heaven and on earth and below the earth to declare, "You are

PARADOXICAL LIFE

Lord" (Phil 2:11), then we would be relieved of the obligation to decide: our appropriate response would be obvious.

But to be Christian means to deal in paradox. It means declaring that Jesus is not simply a dead man of the past but a glorious Lord in the present, even while also acknowledging that his presence now is not one that compels our recognition, and that we are, in fact free to decide whether he is alive or dead, whether he is "our Lord" or not. Our response is not compelled. We are afflicted with freedom.

The readings we have heard this morning invite us into the paradoxical tension, the unavoidable ambiguity of an existence defined by Easter. The readings are intriguing because they both derive from the same community of Jesus's Beloved Disciple. The First Letter of John speaks out of community experience and conviction. The Gospel of John shapes that experience and conviction into narrative. In both readings we find both light and shadow, the truth of divine presence and the truth of apparent divine absence, and the truth of the need to decide which truth will direct the pattern of life.

John's letter opens with powerful affirmation. The message being announced is grounded in actual human experience: they have seen, they have heard, they have even touched! And what have they experienced? That God is all light, and that God has filled them with the light of life through the resurrection of Jesus. His wounds are transfigured by life as he powerfully intercedes for us before God. The blood of Jesus cleanses us from all sins, and we have been called into fellowship with the Father and with his Son, Jesus Christ. There is no darkness here. All is light.

To choose to live by this reality is also to walk in the light. But it is a choice. John says that if we walk in darkness while claiming fellowship with him, we lie and do not live according to the truth. But then, what does it mean to live in the light? John says it is to admit that in fact we do have sin. God is light, we aren't. If we say we have no sin, John says, "we deceive ourselves and the truth is not in us."

Our fellowship in God's life does not mean that we are all at once transported to God's light. We still walk in shadow. We are still marked by sin. We are still dying. The difference is that Jesus lives, Jesus is our advocate with the Father, Jesus expiates our sins and those of the whole world. The light we walk in is his light. Christ is the righteous one, who is faithful and just and forgives us our sins and cleanses us from unrighteousness. Eschatology here does not mean being in light so bright that shadows disappear;

it means having enough new light to be able to distinguish in the dawn and in the dusk between night and day.

The Gospel narrative shows us Jesus appearing among his disciples, who are locked in a room because of their fear. Jesus brings them peace and joy. He breathes on them the Holy Spirit. He gives them the power to forgive sins. John uses this story to draw us imaginatively from the empty tomb and Mary's fugitive encounter to the community's empowerment. This is John's version of Pentecost, by which he shows how Jesus's resurrection is a reality that affects not only him but his followers as well: they experience his presence, are empowered by his Holy Spirit, are sent out by him as he was sent out by his Father.

Thomas is a disciple who missed that community experience. And he is reluctant to accept the testimony of others that "We have seen the Lord." Thomas is a staunch friend of Jesus. He was the one willing to go with Jesus to Jerusalem to face death with him (John 11:16). But he is also a staunch empiricist. He wants Jesus either to be definitively dead or palpably alive. He wants his sense of touch to anchor any conviction that it is really Jesus and that he has really been raised. He wants a fact he can depend on.

When confronted by Jesus and invited by him to plunge his fingers and hand into his wounds, however, Thomas discovers that the mystery facing him is too vast to be anchored by mere fact. This is truly Jesus, all right, but now he passes through locked doors, he breathes the Holy Spirit. His wounds are real, but transfigured. At the sight of Jesus and at the sound of his voice, Thomas responds with faith: "My Lord and my God." As so often in John's Gospel, it is Jesus himself who draws the lesson for those of us who are not part of that first community that could see and hear and touch: "Have you believed because you have seen me? Blessed are those who have not seen and yet believe."

Those of us who gather in the name of Jesus this morning may find ourselves with a bit of Easter hangover induced by too much chocolate and too much liturgy. The excited flush of those early morning appearances has passed. Our life goes on, much as it always does. The readings we have heard are perfect for this moment. They remind us that not even in the time of magical beginnings was everything obvious and clear; that from the start the good news was anchored not by fact but by experience and testimony; that the presence of Jesus was, from the beginning, mediated by a community that breathed the Holy Spirit, forgave sins, and lived peacefully and joyfully its fellowship in the light.

Then as now, it was tempting to seek an anchor of factual certainty. But now as then, faith is a choice to live in the paradox of already and not yet, of the power of life and the persistence of sin, of certain conviction and ambiguous experience, of certain experience and wavering conviction. Now as then, the sea of uncertainty is vast, and the raft of faith is tiny and fragile. But look, we float. We float.

DYING WE LIVE[1]

1 Peter 1:22—2:9

My brothers and sisters in Christ, for nearly two thousand years the words we have just heard have been read to believers during the Easter season. So perfectly does its language fit the experience of the newly baptized, in fact, that some scholars think it was first composed as a sermon to be preached to new Christians at the paschal vigil.

Freshly initiated into the community of the risen Christ, they heard themselves described as "new-born babes drinking pure spiritual milk." They were told that they who had not known mercy had now been shown mercy, that they who had been no people at all were now God's people, called out of darkness into the light in order to proclaim the wondrous deeds of the Lord.

What is remarkable is not that these words were read long ago, but that we should continue to have them read to us today. By gathering in this heap of stones in the middle of this great city to listen together to these ancient words, we imply that these words apply to us no less than they did to those with heads dripping with water and eyes shining from the night turned to day by candlelight, that just as they were true for them, so they are true for us.

But how can we imply any such thing? How can we believe such things about ourselves? Surely you and I know about ourselves how much of our lives are not reborn, how much we remain locked in darkness, how singularly void of mercy are our days, how little we feel part of a people. We have walked here past walls of brick and stone, hard and cold as our daily more private cells. So great is the disparity between the words of comfort—and yes, of sweetness—that we have heard today, these words so filled with the

---

1. Preached at to the Episcopal community at Christ Cathedral, Indianapolis, Indiana, 1987.

excitement of new life that they stumble from one image to another, so great is the distance between these words and our lives that we must ask how we might put them together. How can we even hear them? For you and I have lived through our separate desperate winters of discontent, have grown bitter with struggle, have dwelt in sad decline and died the death of our hopes. We have spent many nights on lonely living room couches. How can these words decipher our lives? And how can our lives interpret these words?

The words we hear read to us interpret our lives in a way that we of ourselves cannot, because they view our lives from a perspective no one of us is able to attain. They tell us that our story of decline and depression and slow death—the story we repeat and memorize each in our closets of fear—this story we tell ourselves is not complete. The words give us a new and surprising ending. Death, we learn, leaps to new life. Loneliness begets community. Despair is conquered by hope.

The words do not tell us how this ending occurs. But they tell us why: because the power of God is at work, darkly, obscurely, furtively, bringing life out of death in our existence and in that of the whole world.

Oh no, we object, do not tell me that! Such a reading is too bizarre. It misses the facts entirely. Look at my despair, how deep! See my wounds, how painful! Observe the death of my dreams, how obvious! Can't you hear the cry of prisoners ringing down the stone walls of this city; can't you hear the muttering madness of our lonely days and nights? These words you speak of resurrection and new life, they are not only obscure, they are silly. Offensive. They trivialize the tragedy of my existence.

But wait, says the words, wait, hear the whole story. No one denies the reality of death and all its smaller simulacra. Winter is real and ices the soul. But did you not look around you as you walked here today? Did you not look up and see the sun, or hear the song of birds or smell the flowers? Didn't the breeze kiss your hair as it did the trees with soft delight rather than deadly chill?

Is this not newness? Palpable, undeniable, inexorable, unaccountable, uncontrollable? Does not the earth *live* beneath the concrete streets of this city, live in a way it did not just days ago? Does it not now sing? From out of the dismal, cold, improbable ground, gelid with doubt, has there not sprung the unlikeliest dance of life? Do not even the solid slabs of pavement buckle and split above the heaving force of life beneath them?

How do we account for all this? We cannot. So long as we dwell in winter we cannot experience spring. So long as we are locked in death's strong grip, we can only remember rumors of past resurrections and hope for future springs.

Is it, then, only a cliche to say of spring that it is Easter, a resurrection in which the world is reborn? No, it is literal truth. The words tell us that it is the God who calls into being that which does not exist who gives life to the dead (Rom 4:17), the God who said, "Let light shine out of darkness" who has shown on the exalted face of Christ (2 Cor 4:6). The stirring of life in the grave of the earth's winter is not a weak symbol. For those who can see and think with the slightest clarity, it is proof. For the God who creates the world out of nothing, summoning Jesus from the tomb is the wink of an eye; calling us to a transformed life a mere shrug.

The resurrection of Jesus signals us that the power by which God renews the world every day is at work in us as well, transforming our mortal bodies into immortal diamond.

The phrase "immortal diamond" comes from a poem by Gerard Manley Hopkins.[2] Hopkins puts the point I am trying to make even more exactly in a poem called *God's Grandeur*, when he writes:

> There lives the dearest freshness deep down things,
> and though the last lights off the black West went
> Oh, morning, at the brown brink eastward springs—
> Because the holy Ghost over
> The bent world broods with warm breast
> And with, ah! bright wings.

The words we have heard read to us decipher our existence by pointing to the greenspot where our life dwells.

How, then, do our lives also interpret these words? By the fact of our coming together here today. By leaving aside all the deceptive side-shows of our culture to hear these words, we make a statement. We declare that we find our true life not in frantic exertion and distraction, but in resting in the deep womb of the world as created by God. We acknowledge that our security is not the result of our constant working but comes with receiving the precious gift of our very existence at every moment from the hand of God.

---

2. "That Nature Is a Heraclitean Fire and of the Comfort of the Resurrection," https://www.poetryfoundation.org/poems/44397/that-nature-is-a-heraclitean-fire-and-of-the-comfort-of-the-resurrection.

Although we come here from separate places, therefore, we join in a common announcement—first of all to each other, and then to all the sideshows who might miss our attendance today and therefore feel to that degree drained of existence. We proclaim that our life is not in the TV news, which is all about novelty and making living things die, but is found in the good news of God's goodness, which creates life out of death at every moment.

We make this statement merely by leaving for these few minutes the carnival of noise and the flicker of artificial lighting from the TV tube, and by coming to this strange and quiet place where nothing much seems to happen, but within whose walls a deep silence breathes.

By coming here, we make the essential, extravagant, gesture of freedom. By choosing to be here rather than somewhere else, we state to each other and to ourselves that the story of human existence as the story of death alone is false; that the view of the world as heading for destruction is distorted; that the joyless posturing of idolatry is a form of slavery. We state together that what heard is also true of us: we are being born although we appear to be dying. And by this simple act, as the words declare, we become a priestly people offering spiritual sacrifices to the Lord.

By ineffable alchemy, we find ourselves transformed even by the simple gesture of coming here together. We not only hear ourselves being called a people who proclaim the wondrous deeds of the Lord, we become that people—all at the same time. Should we therefore wonder how God can create something out of nothing, or bring life out of death, or make us old and tired people newborn babes?

THE EASTER PRESENCE OF JESUS[1]

Acts 2:14–41
1 Peter 1:17—2:10
Luke 24:13–35

My sisters and brothers in Christ, the liturgical readings during the Sundays after Easter keep telling us of this central mystery of salvation within which we stand. It is a mystery so simple that it can be stated in a single line: God raised Jesus from the dead. Yet it is also a mystery so complex that no number of recitals can exhaust it, for the resurrection is not simply a historical event that happened to Jesus in the past; it is equally the experience of God's power today in the lives of those belonging to Jesus.

So, for weeks after Easter Sunday itself, we hear voices from the earliest church witnessing to and interpreting this sudden and surprising good news that had come into their lives because of what God did in Jesus. Hearing those voices, we are also led today to wonder again at how this good news has affected our lives as well.

The first reading from the Acts of the Apostles, for example, has Peter proclaiming on the day of Pentecost that God raised Jesus from the dead, making him both Christ and Lord, and that his hearers know this because Jesus has poured out his Holy Spirit on his witnesses. Peter promises that if they turn to the Lord, they too will receive the Holy Spirit. Those hearing do respond, and are baptized.

Luke then provides us a thumbnail sketch of that first Spirit-filled community: they devote themselves to the apostles' teaching, to the sharing of their possessions, and to prayer. The resurrection of Jesus is the cause, the transformation of their lives is the effect. The lesson is plain: the proof of Jesus's resurrection is to be found nowhere but in the power of the Holy

---

1. Preached at Saint Aloysius Parish, Baton Rouge, Louisiana, 2005.

THE EASTER PRESENCE OF JESUS

Spirit working to change lives within the community gathered in Jesus's name.

In the second reading, the Apostle Peter writes in a letter to Christians in ancient Asia Minor—present-day Turkey—that God raised Jesus from the dead and gave him glory, precisely so that their faith and hope might be set on God. The good news preached to them, he says, is not simply about an event in faraway Palestine, but has and is happening among them decades later: "You have been born anew," he tells them, "through the living and enduring word of God." Their souls have been purified by their obedience to this word, so that they can live lives that are transformed, so that they can love each other from the heart.

In both Acts and 1 Peter, then, we see that the truth of the resurrection is found in the truth about life in community.

But no passage of Scripture better captures what we mean by the resurrection experience than the story Luke tells in the last chapter of his Gospel. We know the story well. We have heard it from childhood and many retellings have only made it dearer.

We might ask why this story is so precious. Is it the quiet mastery of a narrative that provides just enough detail to capture our imagination, and creates the atmosphere of mystery around the stranger who walks as one unknown among his followers and then disappears at the moment he is recognized? Is it the sense of nostalgia induced by the words, "Lord, remain with us, for the evening advances," or the scene of a simple meal at twilight around a fire? These are all reasons why the story sticks so vividly in our minds and why when we hear it read, we feel that we also are present in the story.

It is not only its charm or beauty that so captures us. It remains vividly in our minds because it tells us all the truth about our lives it is necessary to know. We recognize in this story not only the truth about an encounter on the road to Emmaus outside Jerusalem two thousand years ago, but also the truth about every moment of our lives today and every day in Saint Aloysius Parish in Baton Rouge, Louisiana.

The resurrection of Jesus, this story tells us, is more than rumors about an empty tomb reported by some women, and is more than the appearance of Jesus to Peter. It is more than an absence where the body should have been, and more than a momentary experience of someone in the past. The resurrection of Jesus, this story says, is the continuing presence of the living Jesus among his followers forever.

And here we see the importance of the two disciples being so ordinary. Only Cleophas is named; the other may well have been a woman. We never hear about them again after this story. They are not from among the Twelve. They have no standing. They are not the people who make the headlines, but are among the many who read the headlines. Their ordinariness is important precisely because Luke's story wants to show us—remind us—that the presence of Jesus among his followers is freely given and freely available to all. The story's point, if you will allow, is not about the hierarchy but the laity.

There is a reason also why Jesus's presence in the story is so subtle and allusive. He is here and not here. Here but not in the way he was before. The story wants us to imagine his presence in a new way. This is not, "Wow, look, the tomb is empty," a fact verifiable by anyone, or "Wow, look, here's Jesus," as though we could line up for a group photograph with him.

Instead, Jesus is a stranger who rebukes them for their dullness, who points them to the deeper meaning of the law and prophets that told how the Messiah had to suffer and then enter his glory. But they do not recognize the stranger as Jesus until he breaks bread with them, and once they recognize him, he is gone, leaving them as people burning; they say: "Were not our hearts burning within us" when he was talking to us on the road, when he was opening the Scriptures to us?

Luke's story suggests that the continuing presence of Jesus among his followers remains subtle and requires the eyes of faith to detect. It warns us to be aware of how any stranger on any road can and may reveal Christ to us, depending on how we look and listen. It tells us that we can encounter the risen Jesus in this eucharistic meal we share in his name, and in the Scriptures we read together in the power of his Spirit. It tells us to pay attention to each other's stories about the experience of the risen One, so that one of us can say, "The Lord has arisen and has appeared to Peter," and others of us can declare the strange meeting we had on the greyhound bus, and still others can speak of "how he had been made known to them in the breaking of the bread," and all our stories come together in a shared witness to the life that moves among us.

My sisters and brothers, this telling of the good news is especially important for us Catholics in this Easter season, for we have lost the successor to Peter, John Paul II, who after a long time of suffering patiently in imitation of Christ has also entered the glory of the Father.

THE EASTER PRESENCE OF JESUS

Even as we celebrate the mystery of the resurrection life among us, therefore, we understandably also experience grief at our human loss, and perhaps some confusion concerning our future. We can, perhaps, see ourselves in those followers of Jesus who said they had had such hopes before the death of the prophet but now did not know what to believe.

It is entirely appropriate that the faithful spend a period of grieving for their chief shepherd even as they confess and celebrate that John Paul II now shares the life of the God he so faithfully served. Such a period of mourning shows respect and love for the man whose papacy was by any measure historic, and for many of the younger among us, the only pope known. It is thus also entirely natural to think about the future of the church in the absence of such a dominant leader.

What is less helpful to us, however, is to get caught up in the obsessions of the media that have seized on the death of this pope and the election of the next as their rescue for the next news cycle. It is distorting to speculate on the leadership of what the news calls "the largest and oldest corporation in the world" and the pope as "the CEO of the world's largest organization." It is false to think and act as though the papacy was in fact the church, rather than an office of service within the church, and to imagine that the future of the papacy would determine the future of the church.

The future of the church lies, as it has for every generation before our own, not in the papacy but in the communities of transformed people living by the power of the Holy Spirit and giving testimony, through such transformed lives, to the resurrection of Jesus Christ. Popes, whether great or mediocre, come and go. The power of the Holy Spirit neither depends on nor is impeded by popes, bad or good. But the power of the Holy Spirit does need the body of the faithful as the instrument for expressing the power of the resurrected one.

The message of today's gospel—and it is indeed good news—is addressed to each of us gathered at St. Aloysius in Baton Rouge. The gift we have been given is the risen Lord living among us. We are called to recognize him in the stranger, in the Scripture, in the sacraments, and in the gathering of the faithful. No matter what happens in Rome over the days and weeks ahead, this gift, and this call, remain forever the same.

THE CHILDLESS KINGDOM[1]

Titus 2:1–11
Judges 11:29–39
Mark 10:13–16

My sisters and brothers in Christ, perhaps it is only an accident that Father's Day—that child of the advertising industry—falls on Trinity Sunday. Probably is. But we can learn from the curious juxtaposition. Indeed, I will suggest to you this morning that contemplation of the Trinity may be the best way to learn about being a parent.

My suggestion has precedent. You recall that the Apostle Paul tells us that every family, in heaven and earth, takes its name from God who is Father (Eph 3:14). What Paul means by this is that we need to reverse our ordinary process of deduction. We are wrong to learn about God by looking at human parents. That is simply projection. We are, rather, to learn about parenting from what God shows us of himself.

What do we celebrate on the feast of the Trinity, after all? Surely not an abstract mathematical formula. We praise and celebrate the complexity and prodigality of life itself. We pause in wonder at this truth: God is in himself—or in herself, as we remember that all human speech about God is metaphor that reaches only partway—precisely the way God has shown himself to be toward us.

We have learned from the articulate shape of creation, from the redemption won by Jesus, from the Holy Spirit breathed on us, that God refuses the throne of lonely splendor. God reaches out across the abyss of nothingness to create, to call into being that which is not, and God empties himself out to fill that creation and draw it into his own life. From the way God is toward us, we learn who God is in himself: his life is not one

---

1. Preached on Trinity Sunday at First Presbyterian Church, Bloomington, Indiana, 1987.

of sterile isolation but one of fertile communion; not one of hoarding but of sharing, not one of decrease but increase. The One God is not a monad but a living community, a family if you will, in which life is generated, and knowledge and love exchanged, acceptance given and received, in the splendid and mysterious embrace we have learned to name as Father, Son, and Holy Spirit.

And, as we have been given the Spirit of adoption that enables us to cry out, "Abba, Father," and as we have learned that we truly are "children of God," we know that we too have been swept up into this overflowing life which constantly makes room for more life, and we can join Gerard Manley Hopkins in declaring, "He fathers-forth whose beauty is past change, praise Him."[2]

From the contemplation of God's life, we learn about parenting. Our contemplation must always begin, however, with the words that instruct us how God has been among us. Today's three lessons from Scripture provide a frame for our thinking.

We can start with the text from Paul's letter to Titus. A remarkable passage, really, not for its depth or beauty, but for its almost bewildering banality. We are surprised that believers should need such obvious directions. Doesn't it go without saying that old men should be temperate and serious and sensible? That servants should not be refractory or pilfer the silver? That young men should control themselves?

This is not exactly elevated stuff. The gospel here appears reduced to a column from Miss Manners. Strangest of all is the advice given to older women. They are not to be slanderers or addicted to drink. Fair enough. But then Paul tells them, "Train the younger women to love their husbands and children." We blink, then look again. Yes, it does say, "Train them to love their husbands and children." But who needs to be trained to do what nature supplies? Can Paul be serious? In what context could such quotidian, even insultingly obvious advice be pertinent? Apparently, the situation that Paul found himself addressing in this letter.

Paul left Titus on the island of Crete in order to shape up a not very promising community of believers. The church is not only a new one; its members appear to be drawn from a less than elevated cultural level. Paul quotes a well-known proverb concerning the local population: "Cretans are always liars, evil beasts, lazy gluttons." Not a glowing review. We get a sense of the overall quality of the population when Paul indicates that the bishop

---

2. "Pied Beauty," https://www.poetryfoundation.org/poems/44399/pied-beauty.

should not be a violent drunkard, and his children should not be arrested for rioting or profligacy. In a word, this is rough trade.

And Paul reminds his readers that before they were converted to the gospel, they also lived that way: "We were foolish, disobedient, led astray, slaves to various passions and pleasures, passing our days in malice and envy, hated by men and hating each other." Has there ever been a better description of misanthropy?

Paul's point is that gentle love and mutual acceptance are not necessarily the natural state of humanity apart from the good news. It is the grace of God, he tells them, that has exercised a gentling affect on their dispositions. But they remain a people for whom what we consider "natural" attitudes and aptitudes require more hard learning.

Their education into humanity, Paul says, is a result of God's gift to them. He means that the way God has been toward them teaches them how they should be toward each other. He says, "The grace of God has appeared for the salvation of all people, teaching us to renounce irreligion and worldly passions, and to live sober, upright, and godly lives in the world." The Greek participle *paideuonta* here can be construed precisely as "educating us in culture." God's gift itself teaches us how to be authentically human.

Civilization and culture, Paul suggests, are not "natural." They are fragile construction of human meaning that must be learned and be taught. They can be forgotten. In some times and places, fathers and mothers must be taught to love their children.

Here's an example. In the book of Judges, we read the story of Jephthah, and are reminded that not every kingdom has a place for children. Jephthah himself had a miserable childhood. The son of a prostitute, he was kicked out of his home by his brothers. But he grew up to be a mighty warrior for the Lord. His career as soldier-diplomat carved a place for the people Israel out of the surrounding kingdoms. He was devoted to Yahweh and spoke all his words before the Lord.

But to win a crucial victory, he made a rash vow to sacrifice whoever first came out of his house upon his return. It had to have been a member of his family! And it turned out to be his daughter, who met him "with timbrels and dancing." His only message to her was, "Alas, my daughter, *you* have brought *me* very low, and *you* have been the cause of great trouble to *me*." She is the one who must be killed, and he worries about the impact on him. He thinks only of himself. She dies for the sake of his self-consistency and his career.

THE CHILDLESS KINGDOM

The story we have heard from Mark's Gospel, in contrast, tells that the kingdom announced and enacted by Jesus is one that has a place for children. The story has often, and disastrously, been sentimentalized. This is because of the grammatical ambiguity in Jesus's pronouncement, "Whoever does not receive the kingdom of God as a child shall not enter it." The Greek word for child (*paidion*) can either be the subject or the object of the comparison. Usually it has been read as the subject, and piety has sought ways of becoming "childlike," that is, becoming open and receptive and innocent in regard to God's kingdom. As though the point was imitating children. The story as Mark tells it, however, is not about how children accept anything. It is about the way people accept or do not accept children. Jesus's pronouncement, then, should be read this way, "Whoever does not receive the kingdom is the same way he does not receive a child shall not enter it." Notice the structure of Mark's story: the contrast is between the disciples who reject children and Jesus who welcomes them, saying, "Do not prevent them; let them come." And in the very body language of God, he embraces them and says, "The kingdom of God is about just such as these."

We learn three things from this story. First, the disciples represent the tendency of every kingdom established by human measure alone: children need not apply. Why? Because children intrude; they disrupt every attempt at complete control and perfect order. They spoil our neat schemes. They are, furthermore, useless. They demand and do not give back. They are needy without end. They seek a share in our space, and a portion of our possessions. They drain us of time and energy. In a word, they force us out of solipsism into care, from isolation into community. In these ways, children perfectly represent all those in the world we would wish to be excluded from our fantasy of sweet sovereignty: all the wretchedly destitute and elderly and physically disabled and mentally disturbed, all the inefficient and inept, all the bewildered and bothersome. Children, indeed, are the perfect emblem of God's kingdom, which intrudes into our fantasies of a world which we alone control with the reminder that there is another who rules the world and demands of us a response.

Second, we learn that the kingdom proclaimed by Jesus makes room precisely and above all for the poor and the needy and the helpless and the demanding. In the arms of Jesus all the world's children find room. And from Jesus's embrace, we learn the very nature of God. God does not live by excluding the life of others. God celebrates life by making room for the life of others.

Third, we learn that this is the measure that God also applies to us. The way we accept children is the way we accept the kingdom. If we cannot make room in our world for these, who stand for all the helpless and the needy, then we deceive ourselves about seeking God's rule. For the kingdom of God is all about just such as these.

My sisters and brothers, we gather together to allow the word of God to stand in healing judgment on our lives. As we listen to Jesus's words, therefore, we must with painful honesty examine our hearts by this measure. Do we desire a childless kingdom, or do we desire the kingdom of God?

The evidence of the headlines and our hearts alike is not encouraging. We must immediately drop the fantasy that we love children because we have made a cult of youth. That peculiar perversion simply tells us that we want to be children, not that we want to be good parents. The truer evidence might be the emerging pattern showing the way we really treat children in our kingdom, a pattern that suggests more than our protestations to the contrary that we do not accept the children given to us, that we as a society actually hate children.

Let us leave aside obsessive birth control and abortion and child exposure, except to acknowledge that comparisons with the ancient Roman empire grow increasingly embarrassing. Let us simply remind ourselves that what we read and hear of the physical abuse and beating and even the torture and killing of children by parents and other relatives, of sexual abuse by parents and relatives, of child pornography and child prostitution, of the destruction of mind and body caused by drugs, of abduction and abandonment, of education in values left to the random stimulations of a purposeless technology: these things show a pattern, not among others, but among us.

And let us not deceive ourselves. If we seek to establish a kingdom where we exercise perfect control over our lives, define ourselves only by our rights and not by our responsibilities, think only of our careers and not of our call to care, then we are not living by the measure of God's kingdom. Unlike the God we have learned in Jesus, we cannot be bothered.

THE EUCHARIST AND THE IDENTITY OF JESUS[1]

Luke 24:13–35

My brothers and sisters in Christ, the Gospels do not invite the kind of knowing that allows distance and detachment. They demand the deeply subjective kind of learning that requires risk and intimacy. The point of reading the Gospels is not to know about Jesus but rather to learn Jesus as a disciple, that is, to be transformed into the very identity we discover in our reading.

The faithful reading of the Gospels does not ask, "What really happened," but asks instead, "Who is this who speaks and acts now in my life? How can I learn him in the present from this witness and interpretation of his past, written by those who experienced him as also present to them after his death?"

When this sort of truth is sought, there is no end to learning. The most powerful argument for the divine inspiration of the Gospels is that there is no end of learning for those who read them. Although the Gospels yield their surface stories readily to the most casual visitor, they keep giving endlessly to those who dwell in them.

With this conviction, I turn to the passage in the Gospel of Luke that tells of the encounter between two disciples and Jesus on the road to Emmaus, as a starting point for thinking with you about the identity of Jesus Christ in the Eucharist.

Jesus appears as a stranger to Cleophas and another disciple as they make that afternoon walk from Jerusalem after Jesus's execution. He speaks with them about the events concerning himself, interprets Moses and all the prophets in light of his death and resurrection, breaks bread with them,

1. A meditation presented on the feast of Corpus Christi, the Sunday after Trinity Sunday, at a Eucharistic Congress, Washington, DC, 2000.

and then vanishes. For many readers, this is the most beautiful of resurrection stories, more powerfully evocative because of the simplicity and apparent artlessness of its narration.

In this reflection, I focus on the single line concluding the story: "They related what had happened on the road, and how they recognized him in the breaking of the bread" (24:35). The line can be translated more literally, "how he became known to them in the breaking of the bread." This summary statement points the reader back to the climax of the story: "While he was reclining at table with them, Jesus took bread. He broke it and blessed it. He gave it to them. Their eyes were opened. They recognized him." Luke uses the verb *epiginoskein*, "to come to a recognition." We understand this to be, then, as a recognition story, a narrative about learning Jesus.

Here are two puzzles to ponder. First, why didn't they know they were with Jesus all along? Second, why did their recognition come when he blessed bread and gave it to them?

Think for a moment how odd it is that these two in particular should walk with Jesus yet fail to recognize him. They are, after all, "from among them"—that is, disciples (24:13). When they speak about Jesus (to Jesus!) they do not associate themselves with those who put him to death, but with the standpoint of Jesus's followers. They regarded him as "a prophet mighty in deed and speech" (24:20). They had "hoped that he was the very one who was going to liberate Israel" (24:21). They are not just reporting events that happened. They were participants. We understand them to be from among those who had followed Jesus from Galilee and at his execution had "stood a long way off" (23:49).

They were followers, moreover, who had heard rumors of his resurrection. They report how women had gone to the tomb and found, instead of a dead body, mysterious messengers (24:23). They were followers, they were devoted, they had heard of his resurrection. But still they were in despair. They say, not "we are hoping," but "we had hoped."

Why should such as these not recognize "Jesus himself" (as Luke calls him in 24:15) when he joins them in conversation? We could speculate about the physical appearance of Jesus, or the psychological state of the disciples. Luke simply says, "They were prevented from recognizing him." The Greek says, literally, "Their eyes were held in order that they might not recognize him." Two striking things about the construction. First is that this is not something in their control; the passive voice suggests a divine action.

THE EUCHARIST AND THE IDENTITY OF JESUS

Second is the purposefulness of the prevention; the narrator suggests that something was lacking in them that only further experience could repair.

The second puzzle is why they should suddenly recognize Jesus in the act of breaking, blessing, and sharing bread. Aren't these the gestures of every Jewish meal? Why should they remind them specifically of Jesus? This is the puzzle that will occupy us for a while.

We can start by paying some attention to the story immediately before this one, Luke's version of the empty tomb story (24:1–11). It differs in several important respects from the versions in Matthew and Mark, most dramatically in the message they are given. The women are not told to tell the disciples that Jesus has risen and goes before them to Galilee. Instead, the messengers direct them to remember Jesus when he was in Galilee: "Remember how he spoke to you when he was still in Galilee. He said, 'The Son of Man must be handed over into the hands of people who are sinners, be crucified, and on the third days rise.'" And Luke tells us that the women in fact remembered Jesus's words (24:7–8). For Luke, it seems, the recognition of Jesus as "The Risen One" (24:5–6) is intimately connected to the memory of his words.

Does our passage suggest something similar about Jesus's actions, so that the recognition of his presence as the Living One demands the memory of his character as revealed by his bodily gestures during his ministry? I think it does.

Taking the lead from Luke, then, we also can "remember Jesus in Galilee" by rereading Luke's own narrative about Jesus, paying particular attention to how Jesus acts. We seek to understand how the disciples came to recognize him in the breaking of the bread.

As I follow Jesus through Luke's narrative, observing him as a character among other characters, I am struck most of all by his remarkable freedom. This sounds paradoxical, I know, for Jesus also appears to have his destiny determined both by a script provided by Scripture, and by the will of powers over which he has no control.

Even in the course of his ministry, Jesus seems to make few real choices. He mostly seems to respond to what presents itself to him. But perhaps exactly here is where we discover his freedom. Jesus is so defined by his faithful obedience to God that he is freely available to every circumstance. Nowhere in ancient literature do we find a character so accessible. Jesus is approached by everyone: friend and enemy, lowly and powerful, and most of all, by the needy, who seem to intuitively perceive that he can be approached without fear. And Jesus receives them all. Never—apart from those few moments when he retreats for prayer—does Jesus give the slightest sense that there is something more important to do than what he is then doing.

Because he refuses to be defined by any finite plan or project, Jesus is not enslaved by any finite plan or project. Because he is defined by the God who transcends all, because his singular project is to respond to the project of God who chooses—who knows why?—to work out that project moment by moment, Jesus is free to be available to all others in their projects and plans, without himself being defined by them, either. In his being present to every moment gifted to him by God—with every moment's pleasure and every moment's pain—Jesus is at once perfectly faithful and perfectly free.

And, by his freedom, Jesus liberates those he encounters moment by moment. Just as it is remarkable how accessible Jesus is, it is equally remarkable how Jesus does not intrude into the lives of others. He visits their home but does not become part of their family. He remains the stranger, even as he expresses astonishing intimacy. He is present to others, it appears, so that they might be more truly present to themselves. The story of Jesus's visit with Martha and Mary (10:38–42) is the perfect example. He is "at home" with them, fully aware and attentive. Yet we can feel him leaving even as he arrives. And his presence serves to reveal the truth of their presence to each other (in all its complexity), and thereby, to reveal the possibility of a fuller presence to each other because of the (almost accidental) presence of the One who is leaving even as he sits there.

Ancient commentators on Luke's Gospel were correct to understand Jesus's parable of the Samaritan (10:25–37) as self-referential.[2] The Samaritan who risks everything to help the stricken Jewish traveler, who binds his wounds, prays for his lodging, promises to return to settle any further debt, then leaves to continue his own journey, shows us Jesus. The injured man is healed because of the compassionate touch of a stranger. But the stranger enters the injured man's life only to restore it, not to replace it with his own patronage.

Glimpsing Jesus's freedom liberating others leads us to note closely what Jesus does with his hands. We see first that he is accessible to the touch of others. The people afflicted with unclean spirits throng about him and touch him; they are freed of their affliction (6:19). The sinful woman publicly touches Jesus in an intimate fashion and is forgiven because of

2. Origen, *Homilies on Luke*, 34.

THE EUCHARIST AND THE IDENTITY OF JESUS

her great love (7:36–50). The woman who suffered for years from internal bleeding touches Jesus with faith, and she is healed (8:44–46). They touch Jesus, and they are changed.

But Jesus also touches others. When sick people crowd around him, "he placed his hands on each one of them" (4:40). Seeing Peter's mother-in-law with a fever, he "reached out his hand and touches her" (5:13). Coming upon the widow mourning her recently dead son, Jesus touches the coffin and when the young man comes back to life, He "gave him to his mother" (7:15). When called to the bedside of a young girl who had died, Jesus takes her hands, commands her to rise, and, when she gets up, tells the crowd to give her something to eat (8:54–55).

Jesus heals the epileptic child when his disciples are unable, and then "gave him to his father" (9:42). Jesus takes hold of a little child and places him beside himself to teach his disciples about greatness in the kingdom (9:47). He receives the little children when his disciples try to turn them away, and declares the kingdom is all about such as them (18:15–17). Jesus places his hands on the bent woman in the synagogue and liberates her body to stand upright (13:13). When at table with a pharisee and a man with dropsy appears, Jesus takes hold of him, heals him, and releases him (14:4). Finally, in the last free act of his career, at the moment of his arrest, Jesus touches the man whose ear had been sliced off by Peter and heals him (22:51).

What do we see Jesus's hands doing in Luke's Gospel? Jesus does not seize, does not control, does not force. He reaches out to touch that which is broken and mends it. His touch restores people who are alienated by demonic possession, impurity, disease, and even death—he restores them to themselves and to a place in the human community. Twice, in the cases of children either dead or at the point of death, Jesus "gives them" to their parent. In that touch, in that gesture of giving over, I think, we recognize Jesus's essential character.

Luke also shows Jesus at many meals, at which his accessibility is displayed. He shares meals with tax collectors and sinners (5:27–39) and has a reputation for such table-fellowship (7:34; 15:1–2). But he also eats with the religiously righteous Pharisees, who consistently oppose him, even in the context of a meal (11:37–54; 14:1). It was at such a meal in the house of the Pharisee Simon that the woman from the street showed Jesus such extravagant gestures of hospitality (7:36–50).

Three meals in particular help us understand why the disciples on the road to Emmaus were able to recognize Jesus in the breaking of the bread. The first is hardly a meal at all. Early in his ministry Jesus and his followers are traveling on the Sabbath (6:1–5). They are hungry. They are walking through grain fields. It is the Sabbath. The disciples gather a snack as they move through the fields. The Pharisees—where did they come from?—attack Jesus for breaking the Sabbath. Jesus appeals to the precedent set by David: "Have you not even read what David did when he and his companions were hungry? He entered the House of God, took the presentation loaves that only the priests were allowed to eat, ate them, and gave some to his companions. The Son of Man is Lord of the Sabbath" (6:4–5). There is much to think about in this story concerning Jesus's freedom with regard both to the Sabbath and to Scripture, but most of all it shows us Jesus's freedom as directed by the occasion presented by God, here the human need to eat when hungry and the legitimacy of meeting that basic need despite ritual constraints. Most striking to us now is Luke's language: Jesus has David "take the loaves" and "eat," and "give to his companions."

A second meal involving his followers is the open-air feeding of five thousand in a deserted place (9:11–17). Jesus had sent out the Twelve to proclaim the good news and heal. They return with news of their success. Luke connects that mission of the Twelve with Jesus's own by observing that Jesus welcomed the great crowd following them, spoke to them concerning the kingdom of God and healed those in need (9:11). Jesus then feeds the crowd because they are hungry. Luke clearly wants us to see that this great meal for thousands enabled by Jesus's ability to multiply five loaves of bread and two fishes into a feast that has enough leftovers to fill twelve baskets (9:17) as continuous with Jesus's self-emptying service to the people in teaching and healing. It is another example of his hands touching those in need. But on this occasion, he involves the twelve in the table service, just as he had associated them in his preaching and healing. Jesus takes the five loaves and two fish. He looks up to heaven. He blesses and breaks, and then "he gave them to the disciples to serve the crowd" (9:16).

The third meal shared by Jesus and his disciples is the Passover meal before his death (22:14–23). Here is the climax of Jesus's ministry among the people as the one who touched and healed and fed. Now, when Jesus takes bread and gives thanks, and breaks it, and give it to them—the same words in the same sequence as in the feeding of the multitude—his words make explicit what had always been implicit in his body language: "This is

THE EUCHARIST AND THE IDENTITY OF JESUS

my body, which is being given for you." And when he hands them the cup of wine, "This cup is the new covenant in my blood which is being poured out for you" (22:19–20).

Just as the bread and fishes in the wilderness expressed Jesus's ministry of service in teaching and healing, so here the bread and wine symbolize the death that will perfectly express Jesus's identity as God's gift of loving service to humanity. His body—that is, his very self—is being given "for them." It was given moment by moment in his ministry. It will shortly be given totally as he is "handed over" to the death he had so often predicted. His blood—that is, his very life—is being poured out for them.

We should note two further aspects that Luke alone includes in his account of the last supper. The first is his instruction to the disciples who—right after Jesus symbolically hands over himself!—begin arguing about who was greatest among them. He says that authority is not about domination over others but about service to others: "The greater among you is to become as the younger. And the one who governs is to be as one who serves." He spells out this radical view of authority in terms of a meal: "For who is greater, the one who reclines at table, or the one who serves at table?" The answer is obvious to anyone in the Hellenistic world or in our universe of five-star restaurants, and Jesus supplies it: "Is it not the one who reclines at table?" This is, after all, the way of the world. But what is the way of Jesus? He continues, "But I am in your midst as the one who serves at table" (23:24–27). The lesson could not be plainer: those who exercise authority in the name of Jesus must imitate the manner of Jesus; they must serve rather than dominate.

Luke adds one more distinctive element to the meal. After Jesus declares over the bread, "This is my body which is being given for you," Luke has him add, "Keep doing this as a remembrance of me" (22:19). As it happens, Paul also remembers Jesus's words in this same form, when he reminds the Corinthians of Jesus's last meal, "This is my body, the one for you. Keep on doing this in my remembrance" (1 Cor 11:24). Both Paul and Luke have "keep doing *touto*," that is, "this thing." But what does Jesus mean by "this thing?"

Does it mean the ritual of breaking bread in his name? Yes, surely that. But surely also more than that. Surely, Jesus means by "this thing" all that his gesture of breaking bread as his body and pouring out wine as his blood signifies as the gift of his very life in service to others. Keeping on doing "this thing," then, means not only celebrating a ritual but above all living according to this pattern. This gesture, with this meaning, reveals the identity of Jesus within the church. And this is, as Jesus states, in "remembrance" of him.

We come full circle back to our starting passage. We saw that the women at the tomb also were told to "remember" what Jesus had said, and we have remembered with them the characteristic gestures of Jesus that reveal his identity. We remembered especially places in the Gospel where he touched and was touched, and the meals he shared with others.

Now we can understand how the disciples on the way to Emmaus came to remembrance, were jolted into full recognition, when they saw Jesus break bread before them, heard him bless God, and felt his touch as he handed that bread to them.

As in the other stories we have seen, however, Jesus's simple gesture gains context from the other ways he was present to them on their journey. He came as a stranger, listened to their story of early hope, recent despair and ambiguous rumor. And then, as always, Jesus placed himself at their service. First, he stuns them with a rebuke. They are without understanding. They are slow to believe. The problem is not their mind but their will. They do not want to acknowledge what Jesus had told them again and again, that it was necessary for the messiah to suffer these things and enter into his glory.

If they could not grasp what it meant when Jesus broke bread as his body and poured out wine as his blood—if they could not allow into their hearts the mystery of suffering that is the essential identity of the One God sent to bear the world's sin—then how could they recognize the face of the resurrected One in any of his guises?

So, as the risen One who has passed through that suffering, Jesus teaches them once more: "Beginning from Moses and all the prophets, he interpreted for them the things concerning himself in all the scriptures" (24:27). Only in light of Jesus's death and resurrection can they finally understand what Moses and the prophets really meant; and only because they have Moses and the prophets can they discern the meaning of Jesus's path to God.

After teaching them, Jesus wants to leave. But Luke allows him to linger for the meal, so that the disciples, having experienced his presence, having finally understood the Scripture, and having recognized him in the breaking of the bread, can return to their fellows with the news of how Jesus had appeared to them on the road. They do so as transformed people. They say to each other, "Were our hearts not burning within us as He spoke to us on the road, as He opened the Scripture to us" (24:32).

We cannot read passages like this one too often or too slowly, for in reading the story of the first disciples, we read and come to understand our own story as well. We are called to acknowledge all the ways in which we lack understanding and are slow to believe in the presence of the risen One. We are challenged because of our reluctance to face the suffering that lies at the heart of the good news and therefore at the heart of our personal transformation. We are rebuked for the ways in which we seek not to serve but to be served.

We are reminded that as for us, so also for the first believers, the church was a fragile web of experience and story and Scripture. We are thereby encouraged to open our eyes to every stranger who might join us unrecognized on our journey, to open our eyes to the Scripture that shapes our sight, and always, to the breaking of the bread in which the identity of our dear Savior is most clearly now embodied.

TRANSFIGURATIONS[1]

Exodus 24:12–18
Psalm 2:1–11
2 Peter 1:16–21
Matthew 17:1–9

My sisters and brothers in Christ, when we come together for worship, we collude in a playful conspiracy of meaning. We perform gestures from another age and pretend that they are ours. We listen to words addressed to others as though they were spoken to us. And here is what is remarkable: by so pretending and so hearing, we find ourselves clothed with these gestures and words. We return to our own places with something altered in our selves. But only if we don't work at it, only if we can play.

Play has been defined as purposeless but meaningful activity. It is serious but not solemn. Above all, it is not done in order to accomplish something, for that would be work, an activity forbidden on the Sabbath.

So, as blithesome as if we were dancing, we perform these gestures and speak these words. And like really good dancers, we don't need to watch precisely where we put our feet, or focus frantically on the words: the music moves us most when we allow it to sneak up on us and carry us casually across the floor.

The same oblique attentiveness suits our listening to these readings. We know that they were all written for other people who lived long ago and far away. But we pretend that they were written for us as well. We are like eavesdroppers on a very peculiar conversation arranged by lectionary editors we don't even know, a conversation among fragments of texts and echoes of voices.

We listen not only to what each text says but also to what it doesn't say; we fill in the gaps and silences; we try to fit the pieces into a pattern that

1. Cannon Chapel, Candler School of Theology, Transfiguration Sunday, 1993.

none of them alone possesses. Above all, as do all eavesdroppers, "What are they saying about me?"

At first they don't seem to be saying much about us, at all. They seem to be speaking rather about impressive encounters other people have had with God. You know . . . biblical-type encounters, filled with immediacy and urgency and authenticity and self-validation . . . and so unlike anything happening in your life or my life recently.

Moses goes up on the mountain for forty days and nights and "the appearance of the glory of the Lord was like a devouring fire on the top of the mountain in the sight of the people of Israel" (Exod 24:7). Now *this* is what revelation should be like: an unmistakable display of power "in the sight of the people." Likewise in the reading from Ps 2, the kings and ruler who conspire against the Lord and the Anointed One are laughed down by "the One who sits in heaven." He declares, "I have set my king on Zion, my holy hill." Another mountain! Another visible and powerful manifestation of power! The nations are broken with a rod of iron, dashed in pieces like a potter's vessel, as a gift to the one declared by God, "You are my son; today I have begotten you" (Ps 2:7–9). *This* is a revelation anyone could recognize!

Even that fleeting glimpse of Jesus's face on the mountain—again, the mountain—by his disciples, his face shining like the sun, his clothes becoming dazzling white; even that glimpse of glory, though ending quickly despite Peter's attempt at seizing and shaping it; even that glimpse of glory, though concluding with the disciples "looking up and seeing no one but Jesus himself alone"; even that glimpse of glory was in the line of proper biblical theophanies, a revelation of power and authority: "this is my beloved son, listen to him!"

Yes, but . . .

There was a time when I read such accounts simply as records of factual occurrence. This is what happened to Moses. This is what the disciples saw. There was no gap between event and reportage. The narratives were thereby useful for apologetic purposes: here is the evidence that God reveals Godself in history.

But I also sometimes wondered wistfully why such events never happened in *my* life. If pyrotechnics is the paradigm of revelation, I seem to have missed out. Apart from being really happy for Moses and the disciples, and apart from being impressed by the gift of the law and thankful for the declaration of Jesus as God's Son, I was not sure how these texts might reveal something to and for me, might transfigure me.

More recently, infected by the germ of historical and literary criticism, I questioned the events themselves. Surely there was no such fire on the mountain, surely Jesus's clothes and face were not altered in the manner recounted. This strategy enabled me to find some continuity between my life and the biblical story—nothing happened there, nothing happening here.

But it raised other questions. If the narratives are nothing but interpretations, why were they written at all, and why written this way? If not a fire on the mountain and if not a transfigured face, then what need was there for such dramatic stories? Are they exercises in wish-fulfillment, the past of an illusion? Having eliminated event or experience, I seem also to have eliminated interpretation.

More recently still, I have been thinking these disjunctions too severe. I need not choose between event as described and no event at all. The texts, I have begun to think, neither simply *report* revelation or *make it up*. Instead, I have concluded, these narratives *participate* in revelation by their distinctive way of interpreting experience.

This conclusion opened a new line of connection between these texts and my life. Perhaps the process by which those events were understood as the working of God in human experience was no less ambiguous and fearful as the process by which you and I grope for the discernment of God's presence in our lives. Our thinking it otherwise comes from the camouflaging accomplished by narrative. Narrative by its nature creates a false facticity about the past. The past always looks inevitable, even necessary, when recounted from the standpoint of the present. The past always looks objective because it lacks subjects sufficiently free to escape the laws of narrative. Only the present we inhabit is experienced as free, and therefore frightening, when we can decide for discerning in this moment that presents itself either the presence of God or a random firestorm in the hills.

And this brings me to our final reading today, from the Second Letter of Peter. On the surface, it seems to directly challenge the positions that I have so painfully reached. The author is full of confidence concerning the objectivity of revelation as opposed to "cleverly devised myths" (1:16). He gives the example the experience of the transfiguration: "We ourselves heard this voice come from heaven, while we were with him on the holy mountain" (1:18). As he continues, he appears to contradict what I have said: "No prophecy of scripture is a matter of one's own interpretation, because no prophecy ever came by human will, but men and women moved by the Holy Spirit spoke from God" (1:20).

Now, the Greek of this last sentence is notoriously difficult. Does the author mean to say that the prophets did not just interpret events, or does he mean that their prophecies can't be interpreted idiosyncratically by their hearers? Whichever way the Greek is read, however, it seems to contradict my thinking that revelation involves a process of human interpretation. Oh-oh. Here is a voice in the conversation that does not appear to like me or what I think. Worse than that, it turns all the other voices in a certain direction: "You'd better believe it really happened, and really happened in just the way described, because otherwise you are lost in clever myths."

But wait.

When we read 2 Peter more closely, we realize that this isn't really Peter the disciple of Jesus writing and recalling his *own* personal experience. It is a later writer speaking in Peter's name to a generation threatened by a false teaching propagated by those the author calls "false prophets" (2:1). What is their message? That God does not reveal Godself at all, that nothing ever changes, that the delay of Jesus's return is simply further evidence that if there is a god, God is supremely unconcerned with the world's affairs and serenely uninvolved with human lives.[2] It is this sort of position that 2 Peter insists on the reality of revelation through Jesus, and on the truthfulness of the apostles' witness to their experience. They did not just make it all up.

When we think about it, 2 Peter's very insistence suggests the point I am trying to make. Second Peter's world also—it turns out—is one in which even people claiming to be Christian can interpret their lives in terms of God's absence rather than presence, and who can use that interpretation as a justification for living in any manner they please: "I am writing to you . . . trying to arouse your sincere intention by reminding you that you should remember the words spoken in the past by the holy prophets and the commandment of the Lord and Savior spoken through your apostles" (3:1–2). Second Peter contrasts the community's traditional interpretation to their destructive interpretation, opposing a "certain prophetic word" to "clever myths."

Now here is the line I find both most challenging and comforting in the 2 Peter passage: "You will do well to be attentive to this as a lamp shining in a dark place; until the day dawns and the morning star rises in your

---

2. Of all the New Testament compositions, 2 Peter addresses an ideology closest to that purveyed by today's so-called "New Atheists," who have repristinated the ancient hostility of Epicurus and Lucretius toward religion.

hearts" (1:19). A lamp shining in a dark place. Ah. The author himself here pays tribute to the fragile character of his community's story of revelation, or revealing story.

Revelation is not simply a matter of pointing to a flame on the hill and saying that's God talking. It is not so obvious as a voice from the sky declaring a human being to be God's child. It involves rather a trusting in earlier interpretations of events and experiences as a guide to the interpretation of new experience. And in a world that denies any options other than those of scientific verification and delusional fantasy, such a trust seems indeed like holding a lamp in a dark place.

Our faith is a lamp in a dark place until the day dawns and the morning star rises in our hearts. A lamp in the darkness. A lamp holds a modest amount of light. It does not illumine a mountaintop, but it can illumine a room. It cannot warm a city, but it can warm two human hands. A lamp's light is fragile because it is living. It needs protection from the wind. It requires trimming and fuel. A lamp can light other lamps, but only if we are careful and quiet and our hands stay steady. Lamps must be lit one by one to make a larger light. In the case of lamps, fire must be touched to be transferred. And even in the light of lamps, in the moment of transfer, when fire touches fire, more than one face can be transfigured.

The flame on the mountain and the shining on the face of Christ in glory dwells now in the small lamps lit in our hearts that seem alarmingly fragile with all the darkness outside of us and within us. But this is the way we interpret our lamp; here is the story we tell each other; these are the steps of our dance: our lamp will shine in the darkness until the day dawns and the Morningstar rises in our hearts.

CLOTHED WITH CHRIST[1]

Ephesians 4:17–24
Matthew 22:1–14

My brothers and sisters in Christ, we always say something by what we wear. Clothes are not just neutral pieces of cloth we throw on to cover our nakedness. They are, in a real sense, a form of communication.

Clothes definitely do not make the man. Still, what a man or woman wears may indicate what they feel themselves to be, or at least, what they would want others to see them as, or at least for the moment.

When we want to say different things, we can wear different clothes. Think how splendid it is to feel all dressed up with somewhere to go. And when we really get done up in a costume, we can assume a variety of roles. Throw on a long robe and become a Roman senator, or a villain, or Batman. What we wear sends a message.

The message may not always be easy to interpret, because we can dress a certain way for a variety of reasons. Someone may wear a uniform because he is a policeman or because he thinks he is Napoleon. Someone may wear old and tattered clothes because she doesn't care anymore, or because she doesn't have anything better to wear, or because she wants to identify with the poor in a land that is rich.

For others to read the message of my clothing is risky, but for the one wearing the clothes the message is clear. What we wear gives us a sense of identity, with our age group, with our culture, with our profession. They help remind us of who we are and what we are. We wear special clothes for special events, uniforms to play sports, costumes to a party, Sunday clothes to worship. The clothes help us identity with the actions we perform and who we are when we do them. Our clothes signal ourselves.

---

1. Preached on the 19th Sunday after Pentecost to a local congregation in Saint Anthony, Indiana, 1969.

EASTER TO CHRIST THE KING

In today's Scripture readings, we are told that we must also wear a certain kind of clothing to express who we are as Christians, as people who have, however inadequately, answered God's invitation to enter his kingdom.

In his story, Jesus calls it a wedding garment. Like the garments that were offered free at the door for ancient feasts, so also this garment is offered freely. And like the man who refused to wear one of those free garments, yet wanted to hang out at the banquet, was told to leave, so we too, when we refuse to wear the garment offered us as followers of Christ, signal that we are not seriously interested in being a Christian.

Now, it is clear that the wedding garment of which Jesus speaks parabolically is not a piece of cloth we can throw on. There is no single uniform that we can wear which will identify us as Christians. I can wear these vestments or my monastic habit;[2] you may wear a cross or miraculous medal or scapular or religious habit, but these items of clothing certainly do not make any of us Christian. True, they can remind us of what we profess, and who we claim to be. They can stand in witness against our infidelity, but they themselves do not make us anything.

No, the wedding garment of which Jesus speaks is a matter of our hearts, of our drives and dispositions, of our fundamental attitudes and motivations, and of the actions that derive from our heart's directions. It is a manner of living in the world.

The wedding garment we must put on as believers, St. Paul tells us, is one put on interiorly. It is to be clothed with a new identity, to put on a new humanity, created after the likeness of God. This new Human is Jesus Christ. When Paul tells us that we should clothe ourselves with him, he is saying that if we want to be disciples, we must think and act and feel according to the pattern set by the Lord Jesus in his human faith toward God and his loving service toward us. Just as our exterior clothing can express something of our identity to others, so must this interior clothing with the mind of Christ express our deepest identity as Christians, as adopted children of God.

And the mind of Christ within us is this: that we answer yes to the will of God as it confronts us at every moment in the demands of everyday life; to respond with yes to the brothers and sisters who voice, however inarticulately, these demands, often enough in ways that are not at all easy

---

2. When I gave this homily, I was a newly ordained priest wearing vestments for Mass over my monastic garb.

to respond to with a "yes." It means saying "yes" to the Father through our "yes" to our neighbors and our enemies, just as Jesus articulated his obedience to the Father through his loving death for humans. It means to place ourselves at the disposal of others. It means not to cling to our position, our rank, our status, or even our very life, but to empty ourselves of self in self-giving. It means tearing off the clothes and costumes of our pretend selves and wearing the wedding garment that is the mind of Christ.

We do this in the hope that as the Father raised Jesus from the dead and gave him a share in that glory destined for him before all ages, so too the Father will raise us up together with Jesus to new life, through the power of the Holy Spirit. To him be praise and glory forever in the church.

GOD THE COMIC[1]

Luke 23:35–43

My sisters and brothers in Christ, people who are in the business of making other people laugh make a distinction between a comedian and a comic. A comedian tells jokes. A comic thinks funny. Henny Youngman and Bob Hope are comedians who tell jokes, but they do not think funny. Dick Gregory and George Carlin and Richard Pryor are comics. They don't often tell jokes, but they think funny.

Listening to comics, we do not laugh as a way of escaping pain (as we do with jokes) but as a means of experiencing pain. Such comics have learned a secret. It is this: beneath all the booby-traps and sharp edges of everyday disasters and humiliations, there is a truth of a grimmer sort, which is that all of us are dying, every day. If we kid ourselves into thinking we're not, it's a joke. But if we hold ourselves within this truth and laugh, it is comic, which is to say, a kind of freedom, not so far from grace.

God, we have learned to our relief, is not a comedian who tells bad jokes. But God is, as we learn every day to our discomfort, something of a comic, who thinks funny. I mean, God comes at things at a different angle than we do, and, the problem is, keeps a straight face all the time.

Take, for example, today's reading from Luke's Gospel. As good news, it is surely gallows humor. It is hardly rendered less so by our reading it on the feast of Christ the King. Dick Gregory, the comic, has in fact suggested, "If Jesus Christ came back, and was electrocuted, you all would be wearing electric chairs around your necks."

By the logic of the world, there is not a reason in the world for us to celebrate Jesus as a king. On the evidence available from governmental surveys and local lurchings of the heart, Jesus is no more obviously a king than Marie Antoinette, another famous executed executive, is Queen of

---

1. Marquand Chapel, Yale Divinity School, Feast of Christ the King, 1980.

France. And she would not be made more so if Giscard D'Estaing[2] wore a small silver guillotine on a chain. All of which makes it a richly humorous enterprise, the comic dimensions of which are suggested by the Gospel passage, read as gallows humor.

Told as a joke, it would go like this. There are these three guys, two criminals and a nice guy, and they are all three hanged. But the nice guy is the one everyone makes fun of. They hang a sign over his head, "This one is the king." The real rulers of the people, the ones who were even now showing the nice guy who was really boss around here, they parade in front of the gallows. They shout, "If you are a king, save yourself." The three guys start talking. One thief also taunts the nice guy: "If you are so hot, save yourself. And us." The other criminal comes to the defense of the nice guy being mocked and says, "I really think you are a king. Remember me in your kingdom." The third guy, the nice guy, says, "You've got it, later this afternoon." Then he dies.

All three guys die. So why aren't we laughing?

Yes, we say, but it's not a joke. The one thief was right: Jesus is the king. So, we need to look at the man crucified with Jesus as the paradigm of faith. From him we learn what a leap of freedom is the leap of faith. It sees the facts all right. It sees that all three of us are dying, this man as well as us. It sees that it makes no difference that we are guilty and he is innocent, we are all dying. It sees that the rulers in any visible sense are not up here on the stakes but are down there being in charge. Faith sees all this, and in the face of the facts, leaps, and says, "Remember me in your kingdom." This is the leap of laughter. The good thief is the first stand-up comic: "OK, you're a king." And we also say, from his comic perspective, the joke is on those inflated, obscene figures who prowl around as though they were really in control.

Jesus is truly the king because we say he is. We create his kingdom by proclaiming him as king. We establish him as Lord by calling him Lord. We form a paradise by dying with this strange fool and crying to him as we die, "Remember me."

We are all, in the end, crucified. We cannot avoid it. But in the end, there remains choice. We can rail at our death and go out angry. Or we can go out laughing, in the leap of faith, winking and saying, "OK, you are the king."

---

2. Then the French premier.

And if we can die this way, so also can we live. Or at least try to, though it is difficult when the nails are already touching nerves.

But still, we wonder. Does it make a difference, after all, if, innocent or guilty, angry or laughing, leaping in faith or recoiling in fear, they all died, as we all die. And no one has come back to tell us which of the thieves was right. Although there have been rumors.

Which reminds us, even as we proclaim his kingdom, that we do not know its boundaries, and are scared to death even of its nearest border. That we know only enough of its language to place the accents wrongly. That we do not very often catch its humor. We wonder, in fact, if we have even sorted out who is comic and who is straight man in this story. We worry whether we have caught whose humor it is at work in the story. Although we catch some clues. We notice that everyone else challenges Jesus, "If you are a king, save yourself;" we notice that the believing thief says, "You are a king, remember me," and we notice, finally, that Jesus himself says at the end, "Father, into your hands I entrust my spirit."

If we think it over too long, of course, we will probably get it wrong. But that too is all right, because the last laugh is not ours.

SAINTS AND ANGELS

FOUNDATION OF FAITH[1]

Ephesians 2:14–22
Matthew 16:13–23

Today we celebrate the fact that we as Christians have a past, and that our past had a beginning. We are not the first who believe. We have not invented faith. Indeed, we are tiny stones built on a solid foundation. The foundation is the faith of the apostles.

As we in this time of renewal scurry about the task of building and refurbishing the spiritual temple that is the dwelling place of the Spirit among us, as we seek to build up the church, it is critical that we remember that the floor plan remains determinative of all we build.[2] The floor plan sets the foundation, and all we build must rest firmly on its base.

So, as we celebrate today the gift of this foundation set upon the apostles, we remind ourselves also of the mandate that gift carries with it: to build this edifice dedicated to the Lord, we must conform to the pattern set by him. Today's Gospel reading points us toward this realization. But if we are to read it freshly as God's word to us, we need to strip away all the layers of theological and ideological paper that cling to its walls. We must forget for a time claims made for and against the papacy in order to hear clearly the claim being made for a firmer than institutional foundation.

Jesus at Philippi posed a question to his disciples: whom do people say the Son of Man is? This is a question of fact. It can be answered by anyone, with no risk involved. Many voices pitch in: some say John the Baptist, some say Elijah, some say Jeremiah, some say one of the prophets. Their

---

1. A homily for the college students at Saint Meinrad School of Theology, Feast of Saints Peter and Paul, 1969.

2. The period following Vatican 2 was one of feverish reform and renewal in the Roman Catholic Church.

answers are a matter of accurate reportage: "people say." A matter of theory, of opinion. No problem.

But then Jesus poses a much different and much harder sort of question, posed directly to *them*: "Whom do *you* say I am?" Here, there can be no retreat to "*on dit*," "people say." Here is not a question calling for data, information, opinion. This is a question demanding the risk of personal decision and commitment. What is their stance, their disposition, toward him?

To this question, only Peter responds. And on his answer, all Peter's greatness rests. Not because his answer was factually correct, as though Peter had done a better job of assessing the data than the other disciples. No, his answer was great because it went beyond opinion into personal commitment.

Peter did not say, "Well, you seem to have all the earmarks of a genuine messiah-figure, and so probably you might be one." He goes through and beyond evidence. He says, "You are the Christ, Son of the Living God." This is to say, "You are the Messiah for me. I accept you as the messiah. I confess you as God's anointed, as God's child." Which confession for Peter the Jew meant, "I accept you form this point on as the new meaning of God for me and my people and all peoples; my life henceforth is centered in yours."

Peter has grasped that the question is posed as a challenge to his own existence, and he responds with what can only be called faith. He steps past opinion to affirmation; he transcends the babble of words to accept the Word.

And it is *this* response that Jesus calls blessed. It is this response, in this response, that Jesus recognized his Father's hand at work. He saw that God had brought Peter to a place that Peter could never have reached on his own. And it is on Peter's response of faith that Jesus stakes the continuance of his own saving mission, and on which he lays the foundation of the church. The church rests on the rashness and the sureness of faith. It is Peter's faith that brings him the promise of authority within the community of believers, it is his faith that makes him, together with all the other apostles and prophets, the sure foundation on which the church is constructed.

It is not, let us note, Peter's intelligence, talent, or organizational ability that made him the rock on which Jesus could build. Nor, for that matter, was it his fine grasp of doctrinal orthodoxy. Until the Spirit came, Peter had not yet been led into all truth concerning Jesus. What makes him the rock is his simple affirmation that "yes, Jesus is God's anointed for me and for the world." It is this affirmation that opens the world to the saving presence of Jesus. And this is the only authority worth talking about.

Peter surely did not know all that his confession would involve. He didn't even know the most important part of it. But he would learn. He would learn through the hard purgation worked by the word of God in his life.

In the very next passage in Matthew's Gospel, in fact, Jesus himself rebukes Peter for his nationalistic and grandiose idea of what a messiah should be. Surely a messiah worthy of the name would not suffer shame and a shameful death! Jesus tells him, "You are a stumbling block, a Satan to me."

Peter had said to Jesus, "You are messiah to me," and Jesus tells Peter, "You are Satan to me." Every answer we give to Christ leads inevitably to another question put to ourselves. We can say with Peter, "You are Christ to me," and we can expect back Jesus's answer, "You are an obstruction to me. You close the world to my saving presence by your narrowness, your smugness, your comfortable certainties, by your preconceptions and petty notions of what I should be and what you should be." And then hear, "Get behind me."

Jesus's rebuke has a double edge. It means, "Get out of my way, with your foolish opinions." It also means, "Follow behind me where I am going in faith."

And so, we do get behind him, and with Peter, face with Jesus toward Jerusalem, where we will find that the fuller meaning of being God's Anointed One lies in his being the servant of God and humans through suffering and death and new life. And in that position of following in faith, we begin to understand the meaning of our own affirmation of faith, that it also leads in the same hard way to the Father. May he be praised forever.

THE COST OF WITNESSING[1]

My brothers in Christ, it is no accident that the church celebrates the feasts of martyrs so frequently. From the very beginning, the church has recognized in the death of the martyr the closest physical approximation to the self-sacrificing obedience and love revealed in the death of Jesus.

As you well know, in the centuries under persecution, a distinct martyr piety developed. The martyr was seen as the mature or finished Christian, the one who had entered into an almost mystical identification with the Lord through his death. Remember the dissatisfaction expressed by Saint Ignatius of Antioch—traveling to Rome in bondage to face certain martyrdom—that his full realization as a Christian was so long deferred.

Such martyr piety carried with it certain dangers, to be sure. There were cases in which people gratuitously threw themselves in the fire or before beasts and the like. But this was a lunatic fringe, of the sort that haunts all enthusiastic movements. Every truth, we remember, has its counterfeit, and where there is a counterfeit, there is also a truth somewhere in the vicinity.

The core of truth in martyr piety is profound. It is the recognition—built into the term *martyr* itself—that the very essence of Christian identity is to stand in witness, to give testimony to the mighty works of God in creation.

Being a witness to anything important is always a perilous business, filled with risk. To be a witness, we must place ourselves on the line, put our body where our mouth is. When we stand and declare, "I and only I swear that I saw, or heard, or experienced, this and this," we must be prepared to accept the consequences of our rashness, for what we see and hear and experience is likely to conflict with what others want to see, prefer to hear, think they experience. Witness in a context of total conformity is

1. A homily to my monastic community, Saint Joseph's Abbey, 1969, on the Feast of Saint Timothy, Martyr.

meaningless. Witness takes on its significance precisely from its inevitably conflictual character.

If all real witnessing is hazardous, standing in witness to the word of God is even more perilous, for our testimony concerns realities that much of the world is deeply interested in denying or suppressing. Because we speak of realities off-stage and unseen that challenge the things on stage and visible, and because the powers of the world want to keep the conversation restricted to things they can control, witness to the word of God—when it is authentic—almost invariably faces the hostility and resistance of such powers.

The word of God seeks to save the world. But by its nature, that message inevitably places the world in its self-sufficiency into judgment, under condemnation. The word of salvation from God alone bears with it the inadequacy, the counterfeit nature of, all deceptive forms of salvation offered by the world and its ruling powers. The most consistent response of the world's powers to such judgment has been rejection of the Word and of its witnesses.

Such has happened when the Word has been preached with integrity. The authenticity of proclamation can roughly be assessed by how comfortably that proclamation is accepted by the world and its powers.

Martyr piety is not, however, simply about the suffering and death that result from strong proclamation of the Word. This piety perceives the cost of witness in the living out of the good news quite apart from the threat of persecution or prosecution by the state or inquisition.

It sees that being a witness through our manner of life in the world already involves a sort of death. Witnessing by our way of life means living as though the powers of the world were not ultimate, and as though the power of the offstage and unseen God was not only ultimate but immediate and pressing. To live with such a conviction means going out of our narrow and confined selves that are defined by the powers around us and entering into the strange and difficult terrain of God's freedom. It means stepping beyond our private truth into the larger truth that is God. And because we are so constituted as to resist within ourselves such a difficult leap of faith, such an expansion of our horizons, such a judgment on our present preoccupations, every act of faith is in this sense a small experience of death. We die to our self-definition and self-aggrandizement in order to live to and for an Other—whom we never see! Our proclamation of faith in the God who raised Jesus from the dead, then, and our living out of that faith by dying to the delusion of self-sufficiency either of our selves or of the world that wants to construct our selves, is already to be on the path of martyrdom.

The martyr is the pattern of all Christian life simply because all Christian life involves a witness demanding the death (in one form or another) of the witness.

When, as today, we celebrate the feast of a martyr, we remind each other by this celebration that the grace of God is not just an abstract fantasy, but has been a real and powerful force in the lives of actual men and women before us, seizing them and impelling them to a truth beyond their own capacities. When we are in danger of being swamped by the boredom of the ordinary, such a reminder is a good thing.

Made aware once more of the reality and power of God's gift in Christ, we are moved to celebrate the mystery of the first martyr, the witness-in-chief to God's goodness to humanity, our Lord Jesus. And by sharing in the strength given by his body and blood, we may perhaps realize in our small and ordinary lives a bit more adequately the demands—and the cost—of authentic discipleship.

THE ANGELIC HOST[1]

Psalm 103:1–22
Revelation 12:7–12

My brothers and sisters in Christ, my wife, Joy, is increasingly fragile because of age, chronic illness, and the lingering effects of a stroke. Although she is reduced in size and energy, she remains irreducibly the strong woman I married some thirty-six years ago. Sometimes when I lift her from her wheelchair to seat her on the couch, or when I help her down the stairs, she says, "You are my Michael the Archangel."

Naturally, I scoff good-naturedly. "Some archangel," I mutter, as I massage my lower back. I am especially amused when I remember that Joy at some level associates Michael the Archangel with her all-time favorite actor, John Travolta, whose unforgettable portrayal of the heavenly warrior involved belching, smoking, drinking, line-dancing, and battling bulls in Midwestern fields. I admit to scratching my belly the way he did. Okay, and I have belched on occasion. Otherwise, I quickly dismiss the appellation as absurd.

Still . . . I have learned over the years to pay close attention to my dear wife's perceptions. She has earned this respect over a long life of pain, patently endured, a form of witness that has sharpened rather than clouded her insight into the essence of things. I have therefore come to ponder her sometimes surprising declarations. She is my Delphi, my Dodonna.

So, I have been considering at some length her description of me as her Michael the Archangel, especially as I have been thinking about the scriptural texts we use on the Eve of the Feast of Michael and the angels. At first, I must confess, I found little resemblance between my homely acts of lifting and assisting Joy in her daily movements and the book of Revelation's

---

1. A homily on the Feast of the Eve of Michael and the Angels, preached to the Episcopal clergy of the Atlanta Diocese, 2010.

dramatic depiction of Michael throwing down Satan from heaven (Rev 12:9). Michael is mighty and mythic. I am an ordinary Joe. His acts are cosmic, mine are mainly comic.

But then my eyes drifted to the first line of the passage. The seer does not envisage a battle between champions on a field of honor. He sees rather a great war: "War broke out in heaven; Michael and his angels fought against the Dragon. The Dragon and his angels fought back, but they were defeated" (12:7). The war in heaven, to be sure, is a war for the world. The Dragon—who is called the Devil, and Satan, the Deceiver of the whole world (12:9)—seeks to harm God buy hurting humans, and does so by all the means available through warfare on the greatest of all scales.

When we think about what is involved in warfare, we realize that armies are victorious not simply because their warriors are skilled or their armaments superior, although such advantages are not to be scorned. They are victorious above all because all the many thousands of soldiers in the army—the vast majority of whom never hear the noise of actual combat or engage the enemy directly—carry out their assigned tasks with precision and passion.

Far from the realm of obvious heroism, soldiers stand guard, carry supplies, study plans, wash clothes, drive jeeps, prepare rations. They consider every such task essential for victory, and it is. The great weight of allied forces assaulting Europe at Normandy was gathered by the accumulation of countless ounces of effort across nations, seas, hours, years. Without the passionate and precise winding of bandages and assembling of trucks and pumping of fuel, and repairing of radios, Europe would not have been liberated. We honor, and not unjustly, the great leaders Patton and Montgomery and Bradley and Eisenhower. But their leadership meant nothing apart from the moment-by-moment, detail-by-detail devotion of all the angels they directed.

Satan's angels certainly recognize that the war for the world is carried out in just such a systematic and detailed fashion. Satan's angels do not scorn the trivial conquest or the obscure victory. The pimp never passes up a chance to captivate the young and vulnerable, and through them the lonely and lost; the pusher is eager to turn on anyone, however young, to the poison he peddles: retail is fully as acceptable as wholesale. The seducer and corrupter of minds does not care how immature or undeveloped are the minds that are corrupted, any more than political timeservers reject small bribes while waiting for large ones.

THE ANGELIC HOST

The Devil understands that in the war against God fought through the oppression, deception, and captivity of humans, there are no small battles. The meanest murder in a bedroom serves as well as mass murder in camps. The beating of a widow with a stick counts as much as withholding the wages of laborers. The deception of a few in a classroom is as significant as the deception of millions in commercials. The spread of ignorance is as effective as the spread of infection. It all counts. It all adds up. Small victories form large campaigns, individual conquests have cosmic significance.

The same must certainly be the case also on the side of Michael's angels, don't you think? For those who seek to liberate humans rather than oppress them, lead humans to truth rather than to deception, there are equally no small battles. Every small gesture is as important as the most visible and spectacular act, in terms of the cosmic war between good and evil.

Every teacher who grades fairly and carefully even when grades are inflated all around; every pastor who listens to a garrulous old lady as though she were the first and most fascinating old lady the pastor had ever heard; every mother who endures the whining of a daughter telling her all the ways she failed as a parent; every adult who guards the innocence of children against the corruptions of a sexually deranged culture; every friend who holds in secret the shame of another rather than commit slander; every spouse who honors the marriage bed; every employer who pays fair wages; every nurse who watches and prays so long as life lasts; every act of grace and every form of creative suffering counts and has cosmic significance.

It is in this small, oblique, indirect, and humble fashion that I can spot the connection that Joy makes between Michael the Archangel and me. She perceives in the small exchanges and comforting gestures of our life together the presence of a power that is good and is for the good, just as I have learned to recognize in the intense intimacy of aging together the breathing of a graceful spirit. I am no archangel, that is certain. But I understand what Joy means. I am, when I lift her and assist her, joining in the war against neglect and disdain, as a minor soldier in the ranks of the Lord God of Hosts. Any tiny kindness is a glimpse of the mighty kindness that sustains us all. It is in that sense that I direct to you (and to myself) the words of the psalm by way of celebration and reminder:

    The Lord has established His throne in the heavens,
    And His kingdom rules over all.
    Bless the Lord, O you angels,

SAINTS AND ANGELS

You mighty ones who do His bidding,
Obedient to His spoken word.
Bless the Lord, all His hosts,
His ministers that do His will.
Bless the Lord, all His works,
In all the places of His dominion.
Bless the Lord, O my soul.

WE LIVE BY FAITH[1]

Hebrews 11:1—12:2

My sisters and brothers in Christ, I appreciate the honor of being asked to preach to you today, but I confess that I find this sort of verbal hit-and-run difficult. When Wes Allen[2] speaks to you from this spot, his words and your hearing of them arise naturally from the life you share. Wes allows the words of Scripture to challenge both you and him as those words intersect the here and now of DePauw and Greencastle, Indiana. But you and I do not share that common experience, except perhaps, and it is a big exception, the common life we share as disciples of the Lord Jesus Christ. And that is enough for us to make a start.

A wandering preacher must look for other clues pointing to the word that God wants spoken, or at least to be heard, clues drawn perhaps from the way the Scripture passages assigned by the lectionary fall together, or clues derived from the feast in the liturgical year. Today, on this last Sunday of October, several lines converge.

This is technically All Hallows' Eve, the day before All Saints Day, when Catholic Christianity celebrated the triumph of God in human lives among what is called the communion of saints. We celebrate it today, because in our commerce-driven culture, all festivity must fall on weekends. As it happens, this is also Reformation Day, celebrated by Protestant Christianity in commemoration of Martin Luther's challenge to the many corruptions that had arisen in the veneration of the saints. Most familiar to you, this is also the time of Halloween, now second only to Christmas as the most important commercial bonanza in America, the season for silly pranks and tricks even in places outside the DePauw campus.

---

1. Preached to college students at DePauw University on All Hallows' Eve—Reformation Day—1999.
2. Chaplain at DePauw and my former doctoral student.

Intersecting all these sacred and secular moments is the passage from the Letter to the Hebrews we have just heard read, the lengthy and solemn encomium of faith and the practitioners of faith that forms the climax to this magnificent composition's argument. From this complex tangle of associations, your preacher of the day plucks a single phrase for our morning's reflection, namely, "we live by faith," asking of you only that you join me in thinking about the richness of this simple affirmation as we mumble it together on this late October Sunday in the middle of Indiana.

The simple sentence, "We live by faith" describes first of all those of us who have gathered here this morning. We have come to this place because of faith, because each of us has somehow been caught up by realities that we cannot demonstrate or prove yet which for us have become the compelling center of our lives. We come together to express that faith, stating by our gathering this way that we choose to live by no other measure than the one given by the death and resurrection of the Lord Jesus.

And how odd we sometimes appear even to ourselves as we stand with people whom we otherwise would not have chosen as friends, as we pray with words that we ourselves have not composed, as we sing melodies utterly different than those we otherwise hear. How difficult it is sometimes to make sense even to ourselves what life it is that we have by faith. Yet those of us who persist in gathering, keeping faith with each other in prayer and hospitality and singing, find that we do indeed live in a manner deeper and somehow more real than when we, like others, scatter our lives among the shopping malls of distraction that our culture parades before us as desirable.

In our own culture, indeed, we are much like Abraham and Sarah, who said by their faith in a better and future city built by God that these glittering oases of commerce and addiction are neither genuine nor ultimate. By coming to this spare and unseductive space we declare first of all to ourselves and to each other—but implicitly testify to the noisy world as well—that we stake our lives on that life which is real and which only faith can approach.

The reading from Hebrews reminds us also that the pronoun "we" in the sentence, "we live by faith," includes many more than the "we" that gathers in this room today. This "we" embraces all those in every place around the world this Sunday morning who make themselves the salt of the earth and the light of the world by stopping their implicit submission to the idols of acquiring and stockpiling, and turn, as we do, in explicit trust and obedience to the One we acknowledge as our creator, not once upon a time, but at this very moment, in every breath we draw, and so deserves at this moment in the week that we make explicit recognition of what our words and deeds throughout the week ought implicitly to suggest, that we come from God and return to God.

The "we" includes also, as Hebrews reminds us, that great cloud of witnesses who lived by faith before us, who walked before us on pilgrimage toward God, who were tested before us just as we are, who were loyal as we hope to be. It is this cloud of witnesses that the Catholic tradition means when it speaks of the communion of saints. It is not simply that they believed before us. It's that we are able to have faith at all because they had it and showed it and taught it and lived it and were willing to give up their lives for the sake of a city they could not see but about which they had heard a rumor.

The "we" also includes not only those ancient heroes of faith stretching from Abraham to the Maccabees praised by Hebrews, but also the heroes of faith in our own time and in our own lives from whom we have learned of the God who made us and the Jesus who saved us and the Spirit who transforms us. It is indeed appropriate the celebrate the feast of all saints, for we thereby celebrate the victory of God's grace in the lives of real men and women like ourselves over the power of wickedness. By celebrating the saints who lived by faith we give praise to God, whose glory, Saint Irenaeus tells us, is a human being fully alive.

It is Martin Luther, above all, who insisted on the "faith" part of our sentence, "we live by faith." He was shocked, as we should be shocked, by the ways in which religion itself can be turned into a kind of commerce by which we pay in order to get. His rage against the works of Catholicism in his own day was a holy rage directed against deep perversion within the church. Luther rose as a prophet to summon the church of his day—and our day as well—to a faithful and obedient hearing of God's word. He bears witness that faith itself is not a self-generated accomplishment by which we can win God's favor, but always a God-enabled response to the gift that God offers. At great cost and in the face of great danger, Luther clearly proclaimed that it is not trading in the relics of the saints that gives one a share in their company, but only having the same kind of faith that the saints had.

It is a joyful time in the history of Christianity that a Roman Catholic like myself can celebrate Reformation Day, realizing not only how much the Catholicism of the sixteenth century needed purification by faith, but how the church in every day must always be reformed by authentic faith from its small-minded self-interest and its corrupting self-concern. It is a joyful day, indeed, when, on this very Sunday, Catholic and Lutheran leaders heal the wounds of their division by signing together a theological statement on the very issue of faith that first divided them.[3]

Luther discovered the heart of authentic Christian faith because he drank deeply of God's word in Scripture, not as a set of proof-texts supporting doctrines and rituals, but as a collection of dangerous and disorienting compositions that lead us to discover dimensions of faith that go beyond our customary and comfortable habits. If we follow Luther's lead, and look just a bit more closely at the text of Heb 11–12, we also can see three further aspects of living by faith.

I have already suggested the first, indirectly: if our faith is authentic, it will both challenge the world and involve our suffering. The world is constructed, after all, mostly on the premise that God does not exist or reward those who seek God. The world we see around us is structured mostly along the lines of the old beer commercial, "You only go around once; you gotta grab all the gusto you can." The idols of pleasure, power, and possessions compete for our allegiance, whispering that, after all, the one with the most possessions also has the most power, and therefore, the most pleasure.

The only immortality recognized by this world is not a gift from the unseen God, but the consequence of good diet, rigorous exercise, and a fine cosmetic surgeon. And how tempted the church is, in its fear of irrelevance and unpopularity, its terror of disappearing altogether beneath the waves of materialistic competition, to compromise its faith by turning the church itself into a spiritual mini-mall of self-help programs and uplift seminars. Hebrews reminds us that the world does not want to be told that its boasting is empty, that possessions and power have no capacity to give or enrich life, that here, indeed, is no permanent city.

Living by authentic faith does not mean that we end up living in caves or being hunted as criminals, as the heroes of faith in Hebrews were—although we must remember on this day that many of our fellow Christians throughout the world are living under oppression and persecution precisely because of the authenticity of their witness to God's sovereignty. But it does mean that we will suffer the pain of being out of step, of being different, irrelevant, odd, even silly—people who are not to be taken seriously because they claim to see things that the rest of reasonable people do not, claim to

---

3. This was the Joint Declaration on the Doctrine of Justification, signed on October 31, 1999.

hear voices no one else can hear. To live by faith means to be tested and suffer. Indeed, if faith experiences no testing and is free from suffering, we may wonder whether it is actually by faith we live.

Hebrews also points us, second, to the faith of Jesus, the cause of our salvation, whom Hebrews designates as pioneer and perfecter of faith. We most often think of Jesus was the risen Lord, the object of our faith. But like Saint Paul, Hebrews recognizes that the human Jesus was the one meant by the prophet Habakkuk who declared that the righteous one will live by faith (Hab 2:4). Jesus lives with the very life of God now, because as a human like us, he responded to his creator with the trust and obedience of faith. He is pioneer because he has gone before us on the path we must walk. He is perfecter, because he got faith right, once for all.

Hebrews tells us that Jesus was tested, just as we all are, but did not sin, meaning that he remained loyal in his faith, did not turn away when tested in his frail humanity. Even though he was God's Son, Hebrews tells us, he learned obedience through the things he suffered, indicating to us how we also, the people whom Jesus is not ashamed to call brothers and sisters, are to grow in his likeness. By the suffering that comes as an entailment of our obedient faith, we run ever more quickly on the race that Jesus ran before us. We are willing to go with him outside the camp—outside the definitions of the dominant culture—to endure the reviling of a world that thinks us stupid or even crazy, because, like him, we despise the shame of the cross for the sake of the joy that lies before us.

Finally, Hebrews reminds us today why we can choose the terror of falling into the hands of the Living God rather than relax into the comforting hands of man-made idols. It is because God alone can truly give authentic life, and because God is far more faithful to us than we can ever imagine ourselves being faithful to God.

God spoke in various ways in the past through the prophets, but speaks to us now fully in the person of Jesus. If the blood of Abel still speaks, how much more does the blood of our brother Jesus, whose death and resurrection expressed not only the perfect human response of faith toward God, but also God's perfect fidelity to humans in the gift of eternal life.

Today, says Hebrews, quoting the psalm, today if you hear his voice, harden not your hearts. Every day is God's today. God speaks to us every day, calling us to the path of faith followed by Jesus, who is the same today, yesterday, and forever. If today we live by faith, we too by faith shall live.

THE BLESSED AND THE BLASÉ[1]

Sirach 44:1–15
Revelation 14:1–5
Matthew 5:1–16

My brothers and sisters in Christ, perhaps I am not the only one here this morning feeling pulled—even, swept up—into a sort of exaltation at hearing these wonderful texts. Something more than the prosaic conveyance of information is going on in such a hearing on such a day: in the distance, we can hear trumpets and the beat of celestial drums. Here are all the evocative echoes of two thousand years of All Hallows' texts; they do indeed sound the roll.

Sirach summons us to praise famous men. Leave aside whether he should also have invited praise of women. My problem is more basic. When I hear Sirach I forget all about the patriarchs and prophets and think instead of James Agee and Walker Evans walking through the depression-deep South.[2] A bit more riveting, perhaps, is the vision reported by Revelation of the hundred and forty-four thousand—remarkably few, when you think about it—around the throne of the Lamb, happy to have spilled their blood in witness to him. The psalmist continues this motif of exaltation, telling us that the Lord takes pleasure in his people; he adorns the humble with victory. Pretty heady stuff.

Hearing such readings, I am reminded of one of my favorite childhood movies, *The Long Gray Line*.[3] I can't remember much of the plot, but the image has stayed with me: the student-soldiers of West Point were part

---

1. Episcopal Clergy Conference, Dayton, Ohio, All Saints Day, 1984.

2. *Now Let Us Praise Famous Men* (Houghton Mifflin, 1941), with text by Agee and photographs by Evans, was one of the more powerful literary witnesses to poverty in America.

3. John Ford, dir., *The Long Gray Line* (Los Angeles: Columbia Pictures, 1955).

of a long tradition of courage and nobility, another link in the chain that included Grant and Lee, MacArthur, Eisenhower, and Bradley. The movie did not mention the deaths of young men by poison gas in the trenches of Ypres, or of young men burning to death in tanks at Normandy. No allusions either to the shattered minds of young men ruined by war. Only the victories, only the glory, for such is the function of rhetoric.

So also, I think, with these readings we have heard. Gathered in congenial fellowship in this safe place and on this pleasant day, we almost find ourselves nodding assent to the trumpets and drums, and are almost swayed to say, "Yes, Yes," even though we really don't believe a word of it. We don't believe all this talk about celestial victory any more than we believe in the romance of war.

In the church militant, we are the generation of draft-dodgers. We are the disillusioned. We are disenchanted, not just with regard to war and peace, but even with regard to our shared language, the symbols that shape our Christian identity. For us, the words we have read no longer have literal but only decorative content. They are not, we think, the pledge of a real promise, but only the instrument of persuasion.

This makes us, to be sure, cynics. We have taught ourselves to question all establishments, overthrow all structures, demystify all magic, challenge all rhetoric—even our own. We are sadly among the enlightened, and feel ourselves in the dark. We are masters of the hermeneutics of suspicion even when we are not absolutely sure what it means.

For many of us, if we are honest with ourselves, the language of a treasure in heaven, of the crown of glory, of eternal life, of the victory of the lamb, is only empty talk. Some of us have been stripped of illusion by our personal experience: too much of depression, destruction, despair; talk of a future reward seems an easy escape and pleasant fantasy that we can no longer psychologically sustain. Others of us have long ago committed ourselves intellectually to a construal of life that in principle excludes any life but this one. If that means we are no longer Christian, well then, so much the worse for Christianity. We will work to realize what kingdom we can manage for the god-in-process-with-us through changing the evil social structures of this one-and-only world; apart from our efforts at social amelioration, talk of God's kingdom is alienating nonsense. Hope for a heavenly homeland is a form of self-alienation and a deflection from our high duty to this one-and-only world.

In this chastened mood, we listen to the words of Jesus in the reading from Matthew: "Blessed are the poor in spirit, for theirs is the kingdom of God; blessed are the meek, for they shall inherit the earth."

And perhaps we hear even these gnomic pronouncements—these blessings of the messianic kingdom—as we would the slogans crafted by the court jesters of the other kingdom, the commercial slogans that also promise, "do this, and you will get that," "wear this, and you will gain that." No more than we really believe that the right toothpaste will improve our sex life, or a new tie win us a promotion, do we really believe that the meek will inherit the earth.

The evidence, we insist, all points the other way. The aggressive dominate others and colonize the earth and rejoice while they do it. Wherever God's rule might be, we think, it is clear who is running things in our neighborhood. The last time we looked, it was not the meek and poor. It is the loud and arrogant.

Thus, we listen even to the words of Jesus, with sad and divided hearts. We are swayed emotionally by all the fine music, but we are repulsed mentally and morally by the hard realities that seem to confound the music. Or, so we suppose.

And here is the depth of our sad condition: how, we must ask, can we engage the battle without hope of victory? Without the promise being real, why should we—how can we—continue the struggle?

We are much like those new believers in Thessaloniki who, Paul says, were "grieving as those do who have no hope." Why did they grieve? Because they considered their deceased loved ones to have missed entirely the triumph of God because they died before the Parousia of the Lord (1 Thess 4:13). How did Paul console them? He said, stop looking so much at the future. Look more to your present, and what God has already done, and is doing, among you. How can a God who raised Jesus from the dead have a problem with the carcasses of your cousins? Will the God who called—who calls at every moment—into existence that which was not, will such a God pause at a few dead bodies? Our God is a Living God. If you need hard evidence, look at who you now are: you have turned, haven't you, from the worship of dead idols? (1 Thess 1:9–10).

Paul calls them—and us—to a shift in attention. He reminds them that hope is not so much an expectation concerning the future as it is a perception of our present. Or, as 1 John has it, "This is our victory over the world: our faith" (1 John 5:4).

THE BLESSED AND THE BLASÉ

In these beatitudes we have heard from Jesus, then, perhaps to find the blessing we should be looking less at the second phrase, "for they will," and more at the first, "those who are." We rejoice t*hat* there are those among us poor in spirit, despite the fact that our fears and compulsions drive us to possessiveness. We celebrate the fact *that* there are those who are meek, despite the constant threat from fang and claw. We wonder *that* some among us are pure in heart or hunger and thirst for righteousness, despite the ways we are aware of our own double-mindedness and corrupting drives.

The evidence of the promise for which we long, the sign of the victory that we seek, is found, simply, in the *that* of meekness, poverty, purity, righteousness, and, yes, mercy, lived out in real human lives all around us. In a universe of Idi Amins and Gulag Archipelagos, of Hiroshimas and Holocausts, of revolutionaries and terrorists, of systemic corruption and oppression, that there should ever have been a Paul and Priscilla, a Teresa of Avila and John of the Cross, a Francis or Benedict, or that there should be in our lifetimes a Dorothy Day and Mother Theresa and Raoul Wallenberg—or even that this universe contains folk like you and me, struggling every day not to do harm. This is surely evidence of something remarkable. Perhaps we can call it grace.

Such, I suggest, is the victory of God that we celebrate on the feast of all saints. The point is not where the saints of the past are now located, but that they have existed, do still exist, among us at all. That they slog with us in trenches, as you and I do for each other today.

And noting this, we need not flinch at our gathering this way in Jesus's name. For the mark of his Holy Spirit is indelibly at work in those who shoot like sparks of light through this our drab dwelling.

www.ingramcontent.com/pod-product-compliance
Lightning Source LLC
Chambersburg PA
CBHW030114170426
43198CB00009B/618